ENDORSEMENTS

"This book really expands on the scriptures regarding the full armor of God. A helpful explanation of how each piece of the armor works as we choose to put it on, for the battle is real."

—Mary Guzman
Caregiver
Nevada, USA

"A powerful message that every Christian needs to know. In the book Put on the whole Armor of God, William Chandler clearly explains each piece of the armor and its purpose, sharing scriptures that will strengthen our faith. God has provided us with the ultimate protection so we can have a spirit-empowered life and be able to stand firm against evil overcoming any obstacle in our lives. The Word is the sword, the only weapon you need. As you read this book, it will bless you and give a new understanding of God's provision for all believers."

—Irene Stabin
Interior designer
Tucson, Arizona

"The armor of God, is a powerful tool in any Christian arsenal, a daily reminder to intentionally prepare for the battles that rage around us in the spiritual realm. Bill Chandler's description of Paul's teaching thoroughly equips Christians to fight biblically and effectively through applying the full armor of God and by speaking the Word of God for every situation. A must read for those seeking a victorious life over the trials of this earth."

—James and Kelli Marinoni
Oro Valley, Arizona

"I stand in awe of Bill's honesty, determination, courage, and the majesty of his love for the Word of God, bringing it to life for those who will read this book. I also stand in awe of his gentle voice as both writer and teacher with hard-won integrity. God Be the Glory!"

—Claude M. Jones Jr.
Tucson, Arizona

"This book is masterfully written. The anointing of God is definitely upon the author. The insight into the Armour of God is exceptional and awe-inspiring. This is a must read for those desiring to learn more about overcoming the enemy and moving forward in their walk with God."

—Arnell McSwain
Senior Pastor, United Gospel Fellowship
Tucson, Arizona

To Mark Roessler

God bless you in all his Meonyard grace

Love in Christ

W Bonph
5/15/16

PUT ON THE WHOLE ARMOUR OF GOD

WILLIAM E. CHANDLER

PUT ON THE WHOLE
ARMOUR OF
GOD

TATE PUBLISHING
AND ENTERPRISES, LLC

Published by Tate Publishing & Enterprises, LLC
127 E. Trade Center Terrace | Mustang, Oklahoma 73064 USA
1.888.361.9473 | www.tatepublishing.com

Tate Publishing is committed to excellence in the publishing industry. The company reflects the philosophy established by the founders, based on Psalm 68:11,
"The Lord gave the word and great was the company of those who published it."

Book design copyright © 2015 by Tate Publishing, LLC. All rights reserved.
Cover design by Roland Caballero
Interior design by Richell Balansag

Published in the United States of America

ISBN: 978-1-68164-955-9
Religion / Christian Life / Spiritual Warfare
15.12.16

ACKNOWLEDGMENTS

I place all glory and honor to our Heavenly Father and his Son, Jesus Christ our Lord, for the salvation that has been provided toward those who believe.

If it wasn't for the brothers and sisters in Christ who came into my life, this book would never have been written. It's so vital that we learn from one another and become that one body in Christ in good works, deeds, and truth, searching the Scriptures for the answers together.

I have profound respect toward those who labor in his work, near and afar. We should understand that when one labors in his written Word, either by Bible study, preaching, teaching, or just one-on-one conversation, we are furthering his kingdom and strengthening one another. God's Word comes with correction, instruction, and edification. When we receive it and believe it, we are honoring our Lord. All Scripture is given by inspiration of God and is profitable for doctrine, for reproof, for correction, for instruction in righteousness (2 Tim. 3:16).

To my loving wife, which we are joint heirs in Christ Jesus and all the benefits that are provided therein.

CONTENTS

FOREWORD

"Therefore submit yourselves to God. Resist the devil, and he will flee from you" (James 4:7).

Many Christians who should be victorious over sin and circumstances live defeated lives because they neither submit to God nor resist the devil. And many who do submit to God don't believe they can resist the devil, nor do they know how.

That is why this book by William Chandler is so timely and important. His focus on the Word of God and his discussion of the armor of God that we find in the Apostle Paul's sixth chapter of his letter to the Ephesians shows us how we are able to resist the devil.

According to the verse in James above, before you can effectively resist the devil, you must submit to God and to His Word. First, you must be born again, putting your trust in Jesus. When you do that, you become a new creation according to 2 Corinthians 5:17. The old person that you were is dead, and you have a new spirit forgiven and made holy with Jesus living in you by the Holy Spirit.

You then need to renew your mind to the truth of who you are now in Christ and the power and promises you now have in Him as you allow the Holy Spirit to reveal this through God's living word, the Bible. In doing so, you gradually overcome all the old habits and ways of thinking and deceptions of the devil. And as you submit your life to God, you gain the confidence to use the tools God has given us to effectively resist the devil.

Do you want to fulfill your destiny and be an overcomer? Then there is a battle to be fought. But you may say, "I am not a fighter, I'd rather have God fight the battle. I pray a lot, and I'll trust Him to do it." But God's plan is otherwise, according to His Word. Yes, we trust God, but we follow the scriptural pattern discussed in this book.

God Has Given Believers All That We Need to Stand Strong

God has given His Born Again children His Word and His Holy Spirit and all that we need to overcome in life even as we rest in Him from our own ways, living life His way and in His power rather than our own. With God behind you, you can indeed very well resist the devil in your life and in the world.

It is crucial in this day, when the separation of light and darkness is accelerating, that new or immature Christians start becoming strong in the Lord and learn to use the spiritual weapons and armor that the Word tells us we have been given. We need to learn how to live victoriously, overcoming the wiles or schemes of the devil who would try to keep us ineffective.

God's plan is to use each of His children to help advance His Kingdom in the earth, bringing in a harvest of transformed souls from among the lost. Our enemy, God's enemy, wants to stop that at all costs. But we can fulfill our destiny as God's ambassadors if we will learn to stand strong with the weapons and armor that we have been given.

Without the power of Jesus's death and resurrection in our lives, the task would be overwhelming. We have to deal with the world, the flesh, and the devil. And our own flesh can be influenced by the lies of the devil if we allow it. Here are a few Bible verses that tell us what we face:

> "For all that is in the world—the lust of the flesh, the lust of the eyes, and the pride of life—is not of the Father, but is of the world" (1 John 2:16).

> "Watch and pray that you enter not into temptation. The spirit indeed is willing, but the flesh is weak" (Matthew 26:41).

"It is the Spirit who gives life. The flesh profits nothing. The words that I speak to you are spirit and are life" (John 6:63).

"For though we walk in the flesh, we do not war according to the flesh, for the weapons of our warfare are not of the flesh, but divinely powerful for the destruction of fortresses. We are destroying speculations and every lofty thing raised up against the knowledge of God, and we are taking every thought captive to the obedience of Christ, and we are ready to punish all disobedience, whenever your obedience is complete" (2 Cor. 10:3–6).

We can sit back in spiritual defeat and allow the devil to have his way. But that will grieve God, for He has called us up higher.

The Bible says, "And do not grieve the Holy Spirit of God, by whom you were sealed for the day of redemption" (Eph. 4:30). Rather, since we have "put on the new nature, which was created according to God in righteousness and true holiness" (Eph. 4:24), we must live according to that new life "and be renewed in the spirit of your mind" (Eph. 4:23) in order to put off sin so that we "do not give place to the devil" (Eph. 4:27).

When we live not submitted to God but the old way, we are more vulnerable to the ways of the devil. So, first things first, as James tells us, we submit to God before we have the confidence to resist the devil. In submitting to God, we submit to His Word, renewing our minds to God's grace and who we are in Christ with the authority to overcome the evil one.

With the Full Armor of God, We Are Able to Resist the Devil

Then we come to Ephesians 6 and the focus of this book. Once we've submitted to God and His Word and His ways, how do we resist the devil? Ephesians 6 tells us that it is by taking up the full armor of God and taking our stand in it, as it says in the Bible. "Finally, my brothers, be strong in the Lord and in the power of His might" (Eph. 6:10).

We need the full armor of God in order to stand against the devil's schemes. "Put on the whole armor of God that you may be able to stand against the schemes of the devil" (Eph. 6:11).

The enemy would deceive us into thinking our problem is with people. However, we read otherwise: "For our fight is not against flesh and blood, but against principalities, against powers, against the rulers of the darkness of this world, and against spiritual forces of evil in the heavenly places" (Eph 6:12).

And, what should we do? We resist and stand: "Therefore take up the whole armor of God that you may be able to resist in the evil day, and having done all, to stand" (Eph. 6:13).

This book is an easy read and will give you much insight for effectively using the armor of God. Starting out with the story in 1 Samuel 17 of how David overcame Goliath, you will learn throughout these pages to overcome. As the author wrote, "David learned through his experience by the lion and bear that God could do anything through him… We are overcomers, and we have the victory. But we must believe it." This book will help you not only believe, but to effectively resist the enemy.

—Raymond E. Horton
Minister of Reconciliation
Erie, Pennsylvania

Ray has overseen prayer ministries and has been responsible for pastoral care, foundations, and teaching in small groups at several spirit-filled churches for nearly forty years. He writes encouraging teaching and prophetic messages for thousands of believers around the world as a part of his Word of Grace ministry on Facebook.

THE ARMOR OF GOD

The Stone of Faith

You could hear the yelling coming across the valley, the jeers, the laughing and taunting coming from the arrogance of the soldiers massed along the mountaintops. There was a valley between them, which wouldn't hold back an army, but provided less of an advantage of winning the battle if you tried to attack uphill because every commander surely knows that having the high ground would put you into a better position.

Israel fought with the Philistines time after time, and when their champion appeared, they fleed in fear.

From morning to evening, their champion appeared for forty days, twice a day, taunting, cursing, and challenging his enemy. At the end of each day, no one came. And he walked away unscathed by their intimidation. Shaking his head and laughing, "There is no God in Israel! There is no man either. Who will fight me?"

With spears raised and shields rattling together, they felt no one would stand against their power. Who could stand against their champion?

We can find the biblical account in 1 Samuel 17. Let's read some of it together.

> Now the Philistines gathered together their armies to battle, and were gathered together at Shochoh, which belongeth to Judah, and pitched between Shochoh and Azekah, in Ephesdammim. And Saul and the men of Israel were gathered together, and pitched by the valley of Elah, and set the battle in array against the Philistines. And the Philistines stood on a mountain on the one side, and Israel stood on a mountain on the other side: and there

was a valley between them. And there went out a champion out of the camp of the Philistines, named Goliath, of Gath, whose height was six cubits and a span. And he had an helmet of brass upon his head, and he was armed with a coat of mail; and the weight of the coat was five thousand shekels of brass. And he had greaves of brass upon his legs, and a target of brass between his shoulders. And the staff of his spear was like a weaver's beam; and his spear's head weighed six hundred shekels of iron: and one bearing a shield went before him. And he stood and cried unto the armies of Israel, and said unto them, Why are ye come out to set your battle in array? am not I a Philistine, and ye servants to Saul? Choose you a man for you, and let him come down to me. If he be able to fight with me, and to kill me, then will we be your servants: but if I prevail against him, and kill him, then shall ye be our servants, and serve us. And the Philistine said, I defy the armies of Israel this day; give me a man, that we may fight together. When Saul and all Israel heard those words of the Philistine, they were dismayed, and greatly afraid. (1 Sam. 17:1–11)

Goliath was a fearsome foe. Here are some things to think about Goliath's height before we continue.

In 1 Samuel 17:4, it notes that Goliath's height was measured at "six cubits and one span"—about nine feet, six inches. That measurement comes from one Hebrew manuscript tradition, known as the Masoretic Text, a text that was fixed around 100 AD by the Jewish community in Israel. Some think that he could have been ten feet tall, but nine feet is just as intimidating. Other sources suggest this. http://Biblestudymagazine.com/interactive/goliath/

They claim that Goliath's stature grew at the hand of narrators or scribes: the oldest manuscripts—the Dead Sea Scrolls text of Samuel, the first century historian Josephus, and the fourth century Septuagint manuscripts—all give his height as "four cubits and a span" (six feet nine inches, or 2.06 meters); later manuscripts increase this to "six cubits and a span" (nine feet nine inches, or 2.97 meters). http://en.wikipedia.org/wiki/Goliath

Whether Goliath was nine feet nine inches or near seven feet tall, he was a sight to see. When one was covered with armor that came with experience of war, that would bring about fear and uncertainty. Plus a young boy, David, measuring up to him would add a little discomfort. I believe Goliath was nine feet and six or nine inches because King Saul was tall and intimidating himself. His height was higher than any of the people from his shoulders and upward (1 Sam. 10:23–24). So if Saul was seven feet tall, and if the average height was six feet, that would place Goliath's height much higher. As you read on, it gives more details about the weight of Goliath's spear, which shows he was a very large threat. Either way, Israel feared him, and that is clear in the Scripture.

As Goliath appeared before Israel's troops and called for someone to fight him, his sarcastic remarks brought insecurity. It brought fear that weakened Israel into inaction. Saul watched the enemy and wondered what to do, disgusted that no man would stand up and fight this giant.

Saul was very troubled in spirit. What went through his mind? Was the Lord with him?

David heard of these events, and as you read the entire chapter of 1 Samuel 17, you will see what was in his heart. David spoke boldly before Saul after speaking to the others.

> And when the words were heard which David spake, they rehearsed them before Saul: and he sent for him. And David said to Saul, Let no man's heart fail because of him; thy servant will go and fight with this Philistine. And Saul said

to David, Thou art not able to go against this Philistine to fight with him: for thou art but a youth, and he a man of war from his youth. And David said unto Saul, Thy servant kept his father's sheep, and there came a lion, and a bear, and took a lamb out of the flock: And I went out after him, and smote him, and delivered it out of his mouth: and when he arose against me, I caught him by his beard, and smote him, and slew him. Thy servant slew both the lion and the bear: and this uncircumcised Philistine shall be as one of them, seeing he hath defied the armies of the living God. David said moreover, The Lord that delivered me out of the paw of the lion, and out of the paw of the bear, he will deliver me out of the hand of this Philistine. And Saul said unto David, Go, and the Lord be with thee. (1 Sam. 17:31–37)

David confessed what God did for him when he faced the lion and the bear. That built his faith back then, and he remembered what the Lord did for him. When we remember the testimony's of the Lord and what he did in our life, that will inspire us to do greater things all in his name.

This confidence and boldness will harden our steadfastness in his promises. *We will not be moved.* We will stand firm.

> And Saul armed David with his armor, and he put an helmet of brass upon his head; also he armed him with a coat of mail. And David girded his sword upon his armor, and he assayed to go; for he had not proved it. And David said unto Saul, I cannot go with these; for I have not proved them. And David put them off him. (1 Sam. 17:38–39)

Now remember, King Saul was the tallest in Israel, and he tried to put his armor on young David? I bet David couldn't see out with that large helmet on his head or over the mailed armor that he was in. We can imagine most likely he could hardly move in it.

So David said, "I have not proved them." This just wasn't tested in his eyes. He had another armor that he knew that would work.

Saul was wondering about this, I'm sure. Let's see, he said, David killed a lion and a bear? Was this true? Well, one thing was for sure: no one stepped up for this challenge. King Saul might have even smiled and said, "Go with God."

But God was with David.

> And he took his staff in his hand, and chose him five smooth stones out of the brook, and put them in a shepherd's bag which he had, even in a scrip; and his sling was in his hand: and he drew near to the Philistine. And the Philistine came on and drew near unto David; and the man that bare the shield went before him. (1 Sam. 17:40–41)

Here is something that is a little different than what we see in Hollywood movies. Here you have a man with a shield going before Goliath. Isn't it enough, with the giant alone facing David? But David didn't let this concern him; his mind was on the Lord and deliverance was certain.

> And when the Philistine looked about, and saw David, he disdained him: for he was but a youth, and ruddy, and of a fair countenance. And the Philistine said unto David, Am I a dog, that thou comest to me with staves? And the Philistine cursed David by his gods. And the Philistine said to David, Come to me, and I will give thy flesh unto the fowls of the air, and to the beasts of the field. Then said David to the Philistine, Thou comest to me with a sword, and with a spear, and with a shield: but I come to thee in the name of the Lord of hosts, the God of the armies of Israel, whom thou hast defied. This day

will the Lord deliver thee into mine hand; and I will smite thee, and take thine head from thee; and I will give the carcases of the host of the Philistines this day unto the fowls of the air, and to the wild beasts of the earth; that all the earth may know that there is a God in Israel. And all this assembly shall know that the Lord saveth not with sword and spear: for the battle is the Lord's, and he will give you into our hands. And it came to pass, when the Philistine arose, and came, and drew nigh to meet David, that David hastened, and ran toward the army to meet the Philistine. And David put his hand in his bag, and took thence a stone, and slang it, and smote the Philistine in his forehead, that the stone sunk into his forehead; and he fell upon his face to the earth. So David prevailed over the Philistine with a sling and with a stone, and smote the Philistine, and slew him; but there was no sword in the hand of David.

Therefore David ran, and stood upon the Philistine, and took his sword, and drew it out of the sheath thereof, and slew him, and cut off his head therewith. And when the Philistines saw their champion was dead, they fled. (1 Sam. 17:42–51)

This story teaches us not to trust in man's armor nor his devices, for all the experience the enemy may have will never prevail when we trust and stand in God's promises. David learned through his experience by the lion and bear that God could do anything through him.

This is what God is looking for: for anyone to stand against that giant in their lives and to take their sword, and destroy him. Our weapons are not fleshly but mighty through his name. We are overcomers, and we have the victory. But we must believe it. Because of David's obedience in faith, look what happened next. This will encourage others as it is meant to be.

And the men of Israel and of Judah arose, and shouted, and pursued the Philistines, until thou come to the valley, and to the gates of Ekron. And the wounded of the Philistines fell down by the way to Shaaraim, even unto Gath, and unto Ekron. (1 Sam. 17:52)

Because of David's faith victory came to Israel. Because of Christ's faith victory came to the church. We must remember these testimonies in the Bible. And if God helped them, will he help us?

Foresight of the Armor

The armor was the most important protection to have if you were a soldier in the Old Testament times. There were various types.

Most armor would cover vital areas of the soldier. Some kingdoms have armor that would cover the whole man. The parts covered would protect and bring about a defense, which would allow the soldier to go on the offensive as well defensive when attacked.

When he would go into battle, he would have confidence with excellent training, a good understanding of what his armor could protect or not.

The apostle Paul gave us an excellent understanding describing the armor in full detail. Because he knew the Christian would have to face spiritual battles against the enemy.

Yes, Jesus won the war for our redemption when he rose from the dead and presented himself before the Heavenly Father, which completed our relationship in him. But our fellowship with the Lord is our daily responsibility as long as we are on this earth, we will have battles to fight. Or why did Paul write this since God took care of all our battles? The answer is simple: we do have the victory but only if we seek diligently to understand God's armor and not to trust in ourselves and to have faith in his written Word through his Holy Spirit, which gives us this power. You're going to find out by Scripture that God wants you to understand you're in a conflict in this hostile evil battleground, which is the world. Only God and you must work together to conquer the enemy, which is the devil, in your daily life. It's a daily responsibility that we should seek God's guidance.

Let's now explore together, as our brother Paul wrote this message that gives us insight to what he was trying to bring to light.

> Finally, my brethren, be strong in the Lord, and in the power of his might. Put on the whole armour of God, that ye may be able to stand against the wiles of the devil. For we wrestle not against flesh and blood, but against principalities, against powers, against the rulers of the darkness of this world, against spiritual wickedness in high places. Wherefore take unto you the whole armour of God, that ye may be able to withstand in the evil day, and having done all, to stand. Stand therefore,

having your loins girt about with truth, and having on the breastplate of righteousness; And your feet shod with the preparation of the gospel of peace; Above all, taking the shield of faith, wherewith ye shall be able to quench all the fiery darts of the wicked. And take the helmet of salvation, and the sword of the Spirit, which is the word of God: Praying always with all prayer and supplication in the Spirit, and watching thereunto with all perseverance and supplication for all saints. (Eph. 6:10–18)

This chapter of Ephesians will bless us if we have the desire to learn it. Let's cover a few verses at a time and see if we can find scripture in the Old Testament and the New Testament to give references to support each other.

In verse 10 it tells us, "Finally, my brethren, be strong in the Lord, and in the power of his might."

If you will notice, Paul is telling us to be strong in the Lord and in the power of his might. How can we be strong? He tells us it's through his Word by steadfastness.

By reading his Word and meditating on it and grabbing every benefit of the riches within, we make ourselves strong. That increases our faith.

In everything that we do, we shouldn't place trust in man or in ourselves but in the Lord. All glory goes to him. Man at times will fail you, but God will never fail you.

> Be strong and of a good courage, fear not, nor be afraid of them: for the Lord thy God, he it is that doth go with thee; he will not fail thee, nor forsake thee. (Deut. 31:6)

> Only be thou strong and very courageous, that thou mayest observe to do according to all the law, which Moses my servant commanded thee: turn not from it to the right hand or to the left, that thou mayest prosper withersoever thou goest.

This book of the law shall not depart out of thy mouth; but thou shalt meditate therein day and night, that thou mayest observe to do according to all that is written therein: for then thou shalt make thy way prosperous, and then thou shalt have good success. (Josh. 1:7–8)

> Give us help from trouble: for vain [falsehood] is the help of man. Through God we shall do valiantly [force, strength]: for he it is that shall tread down our enemies. (Ps. 108:12–13)

Our enemy is the devil; people are not our enemies and especially not our brothers in Christ. Jesus said in Matthew 5:44, "But I say unto you, Love your enemies, bless them that curse you, do good to them that hate you, and pray for them which despitefully use you, and persecute you."

In the book of Luke, he says, "Behold, I give unto you power to tread on serpents and scorpions, and over all the power of the enemy:

and nothing shall by any means hurt you" (Luke 10:19).

Hurt, in Greek, means to cause an injustice. The Lord has given us power over the injustices of the devil. The Lord wants us to be strong in his promises from his written Word. As we read it, we can either believe in them or not. But it doesn't take away the strength from those words that were spoken by God.

"Put on the whole armour of God, that ye may be able to stand against the wiles [cunning devices] of the devil" (Eph. 6:11).

Paul writes to the church that we need to put on the whole armor of God that we will be able to stand against the cunningness of the devil. The apostle James writes this next point with encouragement, correction, and instruction in the love of God.

> But he giveth more grace. Wherefore he saith, God resisteth the proud, but giveth grace unto the humble.

Submit yourselves therefore to God. Resist the devil, and he will flee from you.

Draw nigh to God, and he will draw nigh to you. Cleanse your hands, ye sinners; and purify your hearts, ye double minded.

Be afflicted, and mourn, and weep: let your laughter be turned to mourning, and your joy to heaviness.

Humble yourselves in the sight of the Lord, and he shall lift you up.

Speak not evil one of another, brethren. He that speaketh evil of his brother, and judgeth his brother, speaketh evil of the law, and judgeth the law: but if thou judge the law, thou art not a doer of the law, but a judge. (James 4:6–11)

The devil is cunning, but we are not ignorant of his thoughts and plans if we learn God's discernment from his Word. This is the escape from Satan's cunningness; when we read and study his Word, we will learn discernment. Also, what we encounter in this world will build our faith when we resist it. Then with this truth as embattlements, we can rest. (According to *Merriam-Webster's Dictionary*, a *battlement* is "a low wall at the top of a castle with open spaces for people inside to shoot through, a parapet with open spaces that surmounts a wall and is used for defense.")

> To whom ye forgive any thing, I forgive also: for if I forgave any thing, to whom I forgave it, for your sakes forgave I it in the person of Christ; Lest Satan should get an advantage of us: for we are not ignorant of his devices. (2 Cor. 2:10–11)

Don't allow Satan to gain an advantage over you. Stand on God's promises. Jesus gave us so many examples of the lies and the traps that Satan and his devils commit. But if we don't read and study his written Word, we will stay ignorant and not have the foresight to deal with the situation.

PUT ON THE WHOLE ARMOR OF GOD

Knowing Your Enemy

> If any man think himself to be
> a prophet, or spiritual, let him
> acknowledge that the things that I write
> unto you are the commandments of the
> Lord. But if any man be ignorant, let
> him be ignorant.—1 Cor. 14:37–38

The world has a saying, "Ignorance is bliss." Not only is this a lie from Satan, but he will try to keep us from everything the Lord has to offer. As it is written in Paul's letter to the Ephesians, it's our responsibility to be strong in the Lord and the power of his might by trusting, relying, and drawing near to God. Believing and acting on his Word.

Paul writes to tell us to put on the whole armor of God. And it's for a purpose.

As we read the book of Ephesians, it's no wonder that all these attributes came from Christ himself. And we have all these benefits in Christ already, which has been provided when we received him as Lord and Savior. What the apostle Paul is trying to do is remind the church what they have—to be strong in the Lord and in the power of his might by putting on the whole armor of God in our mind, by agreeing with what he said on this armor.

God doesn't place that armor on you one piece at a time. It has been provided by Christ over two thousand years ago for his church so you can access it.

You have to make that effort to learn about this armor, and you are doing this by the renewing of your mind through the written Word to comprehend the uses of this armor. Paul covers this with great detail.

These next verses will explain it more clearly.

> For we wrestle not against flesh and blood, but against principalities, against powers, against the rulers of the darkness of this world, against spiritual wickedness in high places. (Eph. 6:12)

Who or what are we fighting against? Paul makes it clear not with physical man and absolutely not with brothers in the Lord in any form. We are fighting against spiritual wickedness, or wicked spirits in high places.

You see, there is no physical confrontation with man but with darkness, spirits, and wickedness. Whether you agree or not, or whether you say God fights my battles, this Scripture tells us differently.

We fight against wicked spirits, and God assists us with his power, council, love, wisdom, and knowledge of his Word all through the Holy Spirit, when we are obedient to its truths.

Jesus won the war, and there will still be battles to be fought, and Satan doesn't feel like he's defeated yet. By viewing the world, we can see that evil and wickedness is still strong.

You can see the battlefield—conflicts in the world and our communities, media, entertainments of the world, and spiritual wars among churches. You name it, sin is still here, and temptations are on a rise, ever increasing. God wants us to learn his Word and obey it to display that love, not just toward God but others also. As we speak the truth, Satan loses a little more ground in our lives.

> Humble yourselves therefore under the mighty hand of God, that he may exalt you in due time: Casting all your care [distractions] upon him; for he cares for you. Be sober [wakeful], be vigilant [watchful]; because your adversary [opponent by law] the devil, as a roaring

lion, walks about, seeking whom he may devour: Whom resist [set over against] steadfast in the faith, knowing that the same afflictions are accomplished in your brethren that are in the world. (1 Peter 5:6–9)

Satan is our adversary, whether we like it or not. *Adversary* in the Greek language, means opponent by law. So don't be afraid, learn God's ways from his Word, and stand against Satan by casting all our distractions over to the Lord.

And the servant of the Lord must not strive; but be gentle unto all men, apt [suitable] to teach, patient, In meekness instructing those that oppose themselves; if God peradventure [perhaps] will give them repentance [change the mind] to the acknowledging of the truth; And that they may recover [to be sober again] themselves out of the snare of the devil, who are taken captive [catch alive] by him at his will. (2 Tim. 2:24–26)

Satan has his own will also—to destroy, steal, and to kill. "The thief cometh not, but for to steal, and to kill, and to destroy: I am come that they might have life, and that they might have it more abundantly [above the common]" (John 10:10).

It's our decision to believe this from his written Word. We either allow too much attention to Satan or not enough. Follow after what Jesus and his disciples wrote all throughout the gospels and epistles and the examples written in the Old Testament.

> And you hath he quickened [made alive again], who were dead in trespasses and sins; Wherein in time past ye walked according to the course of this world, according to the prince of the power of the air, the spirit that now works in the children of disobedience. (Eph. 2:1–2)

Jesus has quickened us, which means we are made alive again. Before we knew the Lord, we were dead in sins and in the course of this world by the prince and power of the air. Satan is called the prince and power of the air, and he walked in the world with disobedience. But now since we have accepted Jesus as Lord and Savior, we are no longer called sinners; we are born again and called saints. But we sure can walk in sin as long as we are in these mortal bodies. We can always receive forgiveness when we truly repent (change our mind) and confess (speak the same thing) our sins to him daily. God loves us, and he will always have mercy, patience, correction, instruction, and encouragement toward his children when they come to him.

Notice, this is a privilege to come to him daily with any problem that weighs on our mind and heart. To confess is to agree with him and admit to him that we are wrong. To repent means to change our thoughts to what his written Word says.

He invited us to salvation; we are sealed by his Holy Spirit with promise. God has made us right with him not by our works but by the finished work that Jesus did on the cross and in the resurrection for our spiritual soul. As believers, we have now the privilege to talk with him and confess what God says. When before we were saved, we didn't confess or agree with God's ways scripturally according to what he said in his Word. And before we knew the Lord, we were by nature children of wrath dead in sins without Christ. Please read Ephesians 1 and 2.

Always be guided by his Word. By reading his Word, we will know truth.

> Wherefore take unto you the whole armor of God, that ye may be able to withstand in the evil day, and having done all, to stand.
>
> Stand therefore, having your loins girt about with truth, and having on the breastplate of righteousness; And your feet shod with the preparation of the gospel of peace. (Eph. 6:13–15)

Paul urges us to put on the whole armor of God, that we may be able to withstand in the evil day. What is this evil day? They understood from the prophets of old and from the words of Jesus himself that trouble is coming to Israel and to the world in the last days. Through the Holy Ghost, Paul wrote that we need to put on the whole armor of God that we might be able to stand in the evil day. For us now, we live for him daily, and some days can be considered evil—the situations we face every day, the temptations, pressures, and unseen dangers. But remember, don't be directed by your fears but by faith in his Word; this is the *armor of God.*

This armor is spiritual and more powerful than any physical type.

It's by believing, trusting, and acting on the knowledge that God gives us through Scripture. The different parts of armor have their purposes. If we don't believe this, then we will not be able to understand it fully.

Girt Your Loins

God desires that we learn to cover the mind with truth. The reality of it all is every day we hear lies, falsehoods, opinions, and rumors that flood our mind. We at times believe what people think and say about us and others, and in return, we will do the same. This isn't healthy, nor is it Christlike.

As Christians, shouldn't we learn to guard and cast down thoughts that reason against his Word? (2 Cor. 10:3–6).

Notice what Paul says below about truth.

> Stand therefore, having your loins girt about with truth, and having on the breastplate of righteousness. (Eph. 6:14)

Loins in Greek means the lower parts of the back. *Girt* in Greek means to gird round about, like putting a robe on to completely cover those areas that are exposed. So what we're doing is covering ourselves in truth. Not what we think or man's traditions, but from what God's Word speaks.

This type of ancient Roman armor would hold all the other pieces together by clips and fasteners, which Paul noticed this in Israel.

Truth must be our primary purpose in our life. If we cling to it, this will hold our lives together. You can never fail with truth, but it isn't always accepted as truth by other opinions.

> Wherefore gird up the loins of your mind, be sober, and hope [expect] to the end for the grace that is to be brought unto you at the revelation of Jesus Christ. (1 Pet. 1:13)

When Paul tells us to gird or to cover our mind, he desires us to be sober and hope, or expect, to the end for grace that is to be brought unto us at the revelation of Jesus Christ.

To cover our mind with his Word is remembering the grace God has given us through understanding the power of prayer and our inheritance in Christ until the revelation of Jesus Christ. This comes by reading, studying, and meditating on the Scriptures.

This doesn't mean you can't have other things from the world on your mind. We will at times while we're here on earth. But don't allow it to control you or to increase those over desires. Don't allow other thoughts to replace God's principles. Don't allow the world to influence you.

God will keep your hearts and minds in Christ, but you must allow him through faith (steadfastness) in his Word to work in you. He doesn't pick up the Bible for us and make us read it. We're the ones who have this responsibility.

Here are a few scriptures on the word *truth*, and you will find more when you study and read God's Word. It's important to understand what truth is and how it will influence us.

> Jesus said unto him, I am the way, the truth, and the life: no man come unto the Father, but by me. (John 14:6)

Sanctify them through thy truth: thy word is truth. (John 17:17)

For the hope which is laid up for you in heaven, whereof ye heard before in the word of the truth of the gospel. (Col. 1:5)

For this cause also thank we God without ceasing, because, when ye received the word of God which ye heard of us, ye received it not as the word of men, but as it is in truth, the word of God, which effectually work also in you that believe. (1 Thess. 2:13)

We can see, this armor that God has provided is very important. Which is Truth.

The Breastplate of Righteousness

The breastplate would protect the chest, the heart, and the vital organs in the body while in combat. If you were a soldier in biblical days, you would have to wear these things to protect yourself in battle.

God's breastplate would protect our spiritual heart, our life within us, and place us in good standing before God because of the finished sacrifice of Jesus Christ when he rose from the dead. God wants us to guard our hearts by learning and reading his written Word.

> My son, attend [give attention] to my words; incline thine ear unto my sayings. Let them not depart from thine eyes; keep [watch, observe guard] them in the midst of thine heart. (Prov. 4:20–21)

God made us righteous not by our works but by his works. We don't feel righteous at times, but if God said it (2 Cor. 5:21), who can argue? This armor shows our right standing with God that we are right with him and pure in his eyes because of Jesus Christ our Lord.

Jesus is forever going before God on our behalf. .

We became right with God and righteous because of one unselfish act: Jesus giving his life, suffering on the cross, then being made a curse on the tree. He suffered in his soul "the pains of death" (Acts 2:24) in the lowest part of the earth, which he and the prophets prophesied. This is covered in more detail in my first book, *Beyond Paradise: The Story of Our Ultimate Redemption.* This book covers the details on the sufferings of Christ.

Jesus's spiritual soul went to a place called paradise, where Abraham and all the saints from the Old Testament went to after they died. But later, to fulfill the three days and three nights, Jesus's soul descended into the lowest part of the heart of the earth. Paradise was in the upper part, in the center of the earth, and there was a great gulf that separated the saved and the cursed. The lost are still in the bottomless pit of the heart of the earth.

Here are some points of this separation on these two locations. See Luke 16:19–31.

Jesus made us righteous with God when God raised him from the dead and took those spirits, also called saints, who were in paradise, with him before God in heaven.

It's by his mercy, grace, and the gift of eternal life, which no man can earn or deserve. We are accepted by him because of his blood and his resurrection from the dead.

And after we accept this free gift, we can walk with him and learn his Word and learn his love toward us, to share our testimony with others. This is what all the men of God did throughout the Bible. They shared their testimony of God.

Here are a few scriptures you might want to consider. They show what he has given us.

> That no flesh should glory in his presence. But of him are ye in Christ Jesus, who of God is made unto us wisdom, and righteousness, and sanctification, and redemption: That, according as it is written, He that glories, let him glory in the Lord. (1 Cor. 1:29–31)

For he hath made him to be sin for us, who knew no sin; that we might be made the righteousness of God in him. (2 Cor. 5:21)

God wants you to know you can come boldly anytime to his throne of grace. He made it possible first to save you by becoming a new creature in Christ. He made you righteous because of Jesus's finished work when he became sin for you.

Then he desires that you walk righteously and be holy, which means set apart to him in fellowship and discipleship. View this as a relationship between a father and his child. And you are his dear child, a child of God, through Christ.

For example, when you were born in this world, you have a mother and a father, and that will never change. You will always be their child. But there will be disagreements and arguments at times, and you won't see eye to eye; it results in divisions between one another. But you are still their child, and they are still your parents.

True, there is no fellowship when there is strife, but if there are peaceful agreements between each other, this becomes fellowship in the family. In the Bible, this is called communion, from the Greek term implying fellowship or agreeing with.

It's the same in God's family; you're born again to be his child. By the oath of his promises from his Word, you are his child. But you at times don't agree with God, your Father. This is called sin. Sin separates you from the fullness of his peace, which is part of the fruit of the spirit. When we don't have that peace, we are not enjoying the full benefits of grace and mercy because of the hardness that is in *our hearts.*

God desires that we have fellowship with him; he will not turn and agree with our behaviors. We must turn and follow him. Then we can walk together side by side. And as a good Father, he will always receive you when you come to him his way, not ours.

Please don't take my word for this. There are many scriptures from the Proverbs, Psalms, and all throughout the gospels on this subject. This is a common principle in the scriptures. We are born again into the family relationship of God as a new creature when we received Christ as Lord and Savior and have fellowship by walking with him daily. This is taught directly and indirectly throughout the scriptures. This shouldn't be hard to understand.

When we were born in this world, we had no decision on being born. Only your parents made that choice, and the Lord knew it beforehand. This example can be described to us how we are born again, having salvation for the soul when we receive Jesus as our Lord.

God made the decision before the foundation of the world to send his Son, to bring us eternal life, to invite us to become sons and daughters through receiving his Son. Having fellowship with God, *it's up to us,* through the spirit of God, to walk in his truth. It's a daily choice.

We are righteous because of Jesus, not because of all our good deeds, and he wants us to walk righteously to follow after his example. If you understand your right with God it's because of Christ, then we walk in his grace and mercy. Then going to him in prayer every day is part of that fellowship, and the benefit is peace within. You will have a sound, healthy mind.

Confessing our sins or acknowledging them shows our responsibility to admit when we are wrong. Praising and thanking him for the victory improves our behavior, and our conscience will be at peace, knowing we can come to God humbly but boldly in the time of need.

These scriptures below are just a few, but they will help us to understand we can come to God at anytime because Jesus made the way to the Father possible.

> For we have not an high priest which cannot be touched with the feeling of our infirmities [weakness]; but was in all points tempted like as we are, yet without

sin. Let us therefore come boldly unto the throne of grace, that we may obtain mercy, and find grace to help in time of need. (Heb. 4:15–16)

So that we may boldly say, The Lord is my helper, and I will not fear what man shall do unto me. (Heb. 13:6)

Come unto me, all ye that labour and are heavy laden, and I will give you rest. Take my yoke upon you, and learn of me; for I am meek and lowly in heart: and ye shall find rest unto your souls. For my yoke is easy, and my burden is light. (Matt. 11:28–30)

The breastplate is very important. It protects our heart and mind. Because, after all, the battle is in the mind. Knowing we are right with God brings peace and rest. It takes away some of the ammunition that Satan will use against us in combat. When we doubt, fear, and don't trust in God's promises, it's a sign that we don't know his words as we should. This isn't to shame us but to be well aware of the enemy we are fighting against. To understand also that we are right with God because of his righteousness that he placed upon us. Through Jesus Christ.

> But let us, who are of the day, be sober, putting on the breastplate of faith and love; and for an helmet, the hope of salvation. (1 Thess. 5:8)

As we can see God's armor is very necessary in our daily walk with the Lord. This reminds us what we have in Christ.

Feet Prepared

> Your feet shod with the preparation of
> the gospel of peace.
>
> — Eph. 6:15

God wants you to protect your spiritual feet by being prepared with the good news, which is the gospel. God's Word will bring peace if we accept it, having ears to hear and eyes to see and a heart to understand. If we speak in arrogance and prideful stance, thinking we know better, we are having the wrong behavior and the influence of a another spirit.

God's Word will bring conviction, correction, instruction, and the edification to our mind and heart when we allow it. When he edifies us, he is encouraging us and building us up by what he wants us to think about ourselves from the viewpoint of the Scriptures.

We are depriving ourselves on what God wants to share with us from other brothers in Christ. I'm speaking about the whole church. We should always be ready to hear and to look into what they have to say but with discernment from God's written Word.

It just might be that God wants to use them to help us to answer our questions and requests before God. We are so ready to reject something when we don't totally agree with it. Listen to what they have to offer and throw out the errors and keep that which is scriptural. God uses his written Word as well as the church to help you with your walk in the Lord.

The feet show clearly our walk with the Lord, and he wants us not to walk in ignorance or in blind faith. God wishes that we walk by faith (steadfastness), believing, receiving, and acting on his promises from his written Word.

Here are a few scriptures that speaks about our spiritual feet and our walk with him.

> It is God that gird me with strength, and make my way perfect. He make my feet like hind's feet, and set me upon my high places. (Ps. 18:32–33)

God makes us sure-footed, like the Deer, or the Rocky Mountain bighorn rams. How does he do it then? By us trusting his Word, believing it, and acting on its promises. Then God will work with us and through us.

> In God will I praise his word: in the Lord will I praise his word. In God have I put my trust: I will not be afraid what man can do unto me. Thy vows are upon me, O God: I will render praises unto thee. For thou hast delivered my soul from death: wilt not thou deliver my feet from falling, that I may walk before God in the light of the living? (Ps. 56: 10–13)

> For thou hast delivered my soul from death, mine eyes from tears, and my feet from falling. (Ps. 116:8)

Thy word is a lamp unto my feet, and a light unto my path. (Ps. 119:105)

> And hath put all things under his feet, and gave him to be the head over all things to the church. (Eph. 1:22)

Now no chastening [instruction] for the present seem to be joyous, but grievous: nevertheless afterward it yields the peaceable fruit of righteousness unto them which are exercised thereby. Wherefore lift up the hands which hang down, and the feeble knees; And make straight paths for your feet, lest that which is lame be turned out of the way; but let it rather be healed. (Heb. 12:11–13)

There are many more scriptures on this. Search the gospels, the Psalms, and Proverbs on this wisdom. It takes time to prepare our walk in the Lord, and it's a daily thing for us all. We at times will blow it, but admit it, and go on. Be at peace with God.

Remember, this is part of the armor; your feet have to be covered by walking in his Word, reading the Scriptures. Remembering those who had a good testimony in God will build our faith, and all the fruits of the spirit will increase. This is God working in us.

Reading about the decisions they made in time of tribulation and trials might give us confidence to walk with God as they did. God preserved these scriptures for us, that by their examples, we could become strong in faith and walk in his steps.

Do you remember the poem "Footprints in the Sand"? Do you remember the other footprints walking by the person's side? They were Jesus's footprints. It shows he will never leave us or forsake us. When there were no extra set of footprints, we're wondering, "Where were you Lord?" That is when we are allowing him to carry us in those hard times.

Jesus carries us in troublesome times when we allow his written Word of promises to be over every situation in our life. That is when he carries us—when we trust, rely, believe, receive, act, confess and walk in his Word.

It's been you walking in the sand all along. And it can be you taking a stand in his promises as he walks through you. For isn't he that is in you greater than he that is in the world? (1 John 4:4). If God is for us, who can be against us? By us standing firm with our feet on the rock, we can't be moved.

What little we understand, God will expect little. What much we know, much will be required by him. This is spiritual maturity.

> But he that knew not, and did commit things worthy of stripes, shall be beaten with few stripes. For unto whomsoever much is given, of him shall be much required: and to whom men have committed much, of him they will ask the more. (Luke 12:48)

This is taught by Jesus in the parable of the talents and pounds (Matt. 25:14–21, Luke 19:12–21). Study this carefully; this describes rewards that we do in this life to the Lord humbly and in grace. Compare it with 1 Corinthians 3:10–15.

When my wife and I were on vacation, we were sometimes going down rivers in Utah. We saw at times Rams on the sides of the mountains standing firm, and it amazed me how confident and sure they were on those rocks. They were so steep, but they appeared not to give any attention to it. They trusted their own abilities. We can place our trust In the Lord, wherever we stand and rest no matter how steep it is.

The Shield

> Above all, taking the shield of faith,
> wherewith ye shall be able to quench all
> the fiery darts of the wicked.

—Eph. 6:16

The Lord unveils through Paul the importance of this shield. God provides this spiritual armor for a purpose: for understanding and knowing his written promises in his Word. When we study, meditate, and read God's Word, this will build up our *armor of faith*. And when you go into combat, you take it with you as a defense against any harm from the devil.

What is a shield used for?

The shield protects you against blows from the enemy in hand-to-hand combat. It also protects you from archers or spearmen at a distance that would attack you to get around your shield to pierce through your armor. This shield that Paul writes about came from the idea of either the old large Roman shields or the oval Jewish shields, which were common in the Middle East by Greek influence.

But I tend to believe it was a Roman shield because these shields were large enough to hide behind in battle, and Paul was most likely seeing those types daily because of the Roman occupation.

This type of Roman shield gave that extra frustration and hindrance to your opponent. He would have to try to get through your shield or around it to attack your armor. If you've ever seen a sword fight in a movie with both opponents having shields, you would notice there would be plenty of maneuvering around to get your opponent off balance and hopefully to find a weak point.

The blows from the sword, spear, shield, or axe on the armor wouldn't necessarily go through the armored shield. But the impact of the blows and force from it would cause shock and trauma. If they got behind that shield, they could attack the body armor, which would bring pressure and eventually break the bones underneath it to weaken the opponent.

There isn't any delay from the attacker if the other isn't quick enough or skilled enough to counter his attack. It's the same between you and your opponent, which is Satan. He doesn't have mercy and is very skilled. He doesn't stop or sleep to rest. He's been around for a long time and has improved his tactics by the millions that have fallen because of his blows.

But don't fear. We have the victory in Christ. Someone might say, "Isn't the war over? Didn't Jesus win the war for us?" Yes, the war is over, but the battles and conflicts still remain as we have seen in scripture. Or why would God speak to Paul to write about putting on the whole armor of God?

And why are those letters that Paul wrote preserved for us to read today? God surely wants us to know and doesn't want us to be deceived. A good warrior respects his enemy and does not take him lightly.

From Scripture, we are going to see that battles continue, and the shield that we are holding will save our life physically, mentality, and spiritually, not by our power, but through his power.

Be mindful that this armor is only for the born-again, saved child of God of his kingdom. God wants all to wear it from youth in the Lord to maturity.

This armor is the nature and ability we have in Christ Jesus, and God wants to remind us that it's been provided over two thousand years ago in Christ. We just need to learn and understand what we have and be mindful of it.

God has given the ability and authority to the believer to destroy all the works of the devil that come across his or her life. Christ Jesus has given it to the church through the knowledge of the fear (reverence) of the Lord and in the name of Jesus, which has been provided by God. Believing and assuring ourselves in the Scriptures, which will prepare and strengthen us in days of trouble.

The Lord speaks about having faith in the Scriptures. Let's see what scripture has to say.

> Now faith [steadfastness] is the substance of things hoped for, the evidence of things not seen. For by it the elders obtained a good report. Through faith we understand that the worlds were framed by the word of God, so that things which are seen were not made of things which do appear. (Heb. 11:1–3)

God's Word formed and framed the worlds, our solar system, our earth, and the atmosphere. Faith is something we can't see or feel with our natural senses. You can't reason it out. To our natural minds, it isn't real. But through speaking his written Word, faith creates something that wasn't there before. Faith is the substance of things you can't see. God would invite men to do his will, and as you read the Scriptures, you can understand how some of their faith was weak. Then as they grew stronger in faith, they would achieve a good result by trusting God and relying on him, thus becoming an elder of steadfastness in the promises of God, by believing and trusting in him. Consider what Paul said about faith and trusting God.

> But they have not all obeyed the gospel. "For Esaias saith, Lord, who hath believed our report? So then faith cometh by hearing, and hearing by the word of God" (Rom. 10: 16–17).

But without faith it is impossible to please him: for he that comes to God must believe that he is, and that he rewards them that diligently seek him. (Heb. 11:6, KJV)

Let's find a few scriptures that is written about the armor and being in warfare.

But let us, who are of the day, be sober, putting on the breastplate of faith and love; and for an helmet, the hope of salvation. (1 Thess. 5:8)

Forasmuch then as Christ hath suffered for us in the flesh, arm yourselves likewise with the same mind: for he that hath suffered in the flesh hath ceased from sin. (1 Pet. 4:1)

Thou therefore, my son, be strong [to make powerful inwardly] in the grace that is in Christ Jesus. And the things that thou hast heard of me among many witnesses, the same commit thou to faithful men, who shall be able to teach others also. Thou therefore endure hardness [to suffer, hold up under evil], as a good soldier of Jesus Christ. No man that wars entangle (entangles self) himself with the affairs [affairs, business, matter] of this life; that he may please him who hath chosen him to be a soldier. (2 Tim. 2:1–4)

In 2 Timothy 2, the scriptures says, "endure hardness," which means in Greek "to suffer, hold up under evil." This makes us to understand we will go through problems in this life, which will increase our faith. By trusting in God's Word brings deliverance, just as a potter uses fire to form his pottery. God's hands form us as we trust in his written Word. If we place our confidence in God and in his written Word and not in ourselves, we will have the victory by the tribulation we endure, and through God's Word, we are formed and strengthened.

These are just a few scriptures that show there is a conflict. Satan has declared war on believers in Christ. So if we are at war with Satan, what should we do? Is this armor unnecessary then? Is this just to put on a good show of strength?

It's for your battle with the devil and his unclean spirits. It's for your protection, and it's time that we take up our shield and stand in faith on what God has promised to us from his written Word.

> Submit yourselves therefore to God. Resist the devil, and he will flee from you. Draw nigh to God, and he will draw nigh to you. Cleanse your hands, ye sinners; and purify your hearts, ye double minded. (James 4:7–8)

What is very interesting is Satan will flee from you. Satan at one time was called Lucifer. He was beautiful, powerful, and wise. An angel of light, he once was known as, "the anointed cherub that covereth." He was created before the world was created, along with the other angels. Lucifer had his position and honor before God the father but because of pride and many other things, he lost it all (Isa. 14:12–15, Ezek. 28:14–17, Matt. 25:41). Can you imagine, he has to submit to you in the name of God's Son, Jesus? How degrading it must be to him and how angry he must be. So you can understand how much he hates the church and will do anything to keep us from the knowledge of God.

If we draw near to God and the authority of his Word, Satan has to flee. Darkness hates light. God's Word cleans us and brings light, and it also places our mind on God and not on our own selfishness.

Keep your shield up, which is faith in the Lord, not in ourselves. Here are a few scriptures on this.

> But thou, O Lord, art a shield for me; my glory, and the lifter up of mine head. I cried unto the Lord with my voice, and he heard me out of his holy hill. Selah. I laid me down and slept; I awaked; for the Lord sustained me. I will not be afraid of ten thousands of

people, that have set themselves against me round about. (Ps. 3:3–6)

For thou, Lord, wilt bless the righteous; with favour wilt thou compass him as with a shield. (Ps. 5:12)

The Lord is my strength and my shield; my heart trusted in him, and I am helped: therefore my heart greatly rejoiceth; and with my song will I praise him. (Ps. 28:7)

He shall cover thee with his feathers, and under his wings shalt thou trust: his truth shall be thy shield and buckler. (Ps. 91:4)

For the Lord God is a sun and shield: the Lord will give grace and glory: no good thing will he withhold from them that walk uprightly. (Ps. 84:11)

The Helmet of Salvation

And take the helmet of salvation.

—Eph 6: 17

The mind is where the battle begins, and it's under the helmet. The way for us to have the victory is to cast down thoughts that don't agree with God's written Word. This scripture explains it.

> For though we walk in the flesh, we do not war after the flesh: (For the weapons of our warfare are not carnal, but mighty through God to the pulling down of strong holds); Casting down imaginations [reasonings], and every high thing that exalteth itself against the knowledge of God, and bringing into captivity every thought to the obedience of Christ; And having in a readiness to revenge all

disobedience, when your obedience is fulfilled.

Do ye look on things after the outward appearance? If any man trust to himself that he is Christ's, let him of himself think this again, that, as he is Christ's, even so are we Christ's. (2 Cor. 10:3–7)

Our warfare isn't in the flesh but in the spirit—against unclean spirits and wickedness. The Lord wants us to cast down imaginations. This word *imagination*, *logismos* in Greek, means reasonings. God doesn't want us to try to figure out what he wants but to read it and believe what is written in his Holy Word.

He wants us to understand and adhere to his reasoning, not ours.

Here is an example.

Come now, and let us reason together, saith the Lord: though your sins be as scarlet, they shall be as white as snow;

> though they be red like crimson, they
> shall be as wool. (Isa. 1:18)

This word, *reason*, is *yakach* in Hebrew; it means to prove, decide, judge, rebuke, reprove, correct, be right. God is pointing out a truth in this scripture, describing their condition, then the solution. So we shouldn't trust our imaginations (reasonings) but his. We face this battle every day; these thoughts enter into our mind. We need to *cast down those thoughts* and replace them with scripture on the problem we are facing. If you have fear, search for scriptures for combat; then read them and get them into your heart. Do the same for any attack that you may face in the mind. Then rest in that knowledge.

Once you quote it to the devil, just as Jesus did, rest in his strength and confidence, confessing a good confession of faith on what his written Word says. Satan will leave you, for a while and those thoughts will not seem to have the power as they did before. Consider Paul's example.

And lest I should be exalted above measure through the abundance of the revelations, there was given to me a thorn in the flesh, the messenger of Satan to buffet me, lest I should be exalted above measure.

For this thing I besought the Lord thrice, that it might depart from me.

And he said unto me, My grace is sufficient for thee: for my strength is made perfect in weakness. Most gladly therefore will I rather glory in my infirmities, that the power of Christ may rest upon me. Therefore I take pleasure in infirmities, in reproaches, in necessities, in persecutions, in distresses for Christ's sake: for when I am weak, then am I strong. (2 Cor. 12:7–10)

Notice the Lord said, "My grace is sufficient for you." His grace and strength is the confidence. We can't do a thing by ourselves. It's him and us working together. Knowing when we are weak, we become strong because his promises never fail. And we take pleasure what comes with it— as being a Christian, not regret it.

The helmet is very vital on our armor. In those days, when they wore it, it was at times heavy and cumbersome. It was necessary to keep you alive, and it kept your head where it belonged. If a soldier lost his helmet, usually it wasn't a good thing. The soldier would have to take extra care when the enemy came against him.

This helmet for the church, in which the apostle Paul speaks of, is salvation through Jesus Christ when we believed on him, and it doesn't end there. God wants you to remember that this helmet is on your head on a daily basis.

We have the confidence and assurance that our soul is saved. Also, this helmet is for our protection in deliverance spiritually, which covers our mind.

The weapons of the enemy will try to work on your mind and make you think your helmet is coming loose or is already off, making you doubt your salvation. That is the first attack Satan uses on every believer when they come to Christ. Satan will give every excuse and every false teaching, using scriptures to do so. If he can be successful to change your mind, lying to you, saying "You lost your salvation this time, and you're a terrible sinner," then he will bring doubt and condemnation. Or he will say, "Why would God have anything to do with you being the way you are?" Cleverly Satan will also try this, "Don't you know if you break his commandments, you will not have eternal life?" Satan will use every trick and tactic to make you feel ashamed and unsteady. He will use the scriptures against you.

If Satan preached to Jesus while being tempted in the wilderness, don't you think he is going to tempt you? If he can corrupt our thoughts, then he will attack the rest of our armor just as well. Then use the commandments of men and their traditions to shut the prison door. Consider what Paul said here.

> But I fear, lest by any means, as the serpent beguiled Eve through his subtilty, so your minds should be corrupted from the simplicity that is in Christ. (2 Cor. 11:3)

Paul is saying, this is simple! The truth that Christ Jesus taught was simple!

We must be assured that our salvation is secure, safe, sealed, and protected by Jesus Christ alone. By his power, not by our performance or works of any kind. It wasn't your faith that brought redemption, but the grace through Jesus's faith (Gal. 2:20–21).

We did believe the gospel that was preached to us which was by faith. But because of Jesus' steadfastness, it was his faith that provided eternal life.

Take what you heard from the written Word and believe what he did by adding to your faith, [steadfastness] trusting in his finished work and by hearing and believing God's Word on salvation to have eternal life. Then stand firm.

Don't go by how you feel or reason it out with logic. We didn't physically die on the cross and became a curse. We didn't pay the price for the judgment of sin. Jesus did. Just relax. Our salvation has been paid for. We can rest in his promises, and our mind can be at peace. And when we blow it, admit it and go on. Don't let fear and condemnation corrupt your mind. Be honest to yourself and to God.

Rest from fear, doubt, and any earthly requirement that you can imagine. It's by the fears of men that these teachings are embraced. By taking one word or a few sentences from the Bible, it develops into a doctrine because of ignorance not studying the whole chapter or principles that the writer intended.

We must use discernment and rightly divide the word of truth. At times, we do err from his principles and commandments, but we can change our mind to what the scriptures teach. Just agree with God and what he says.

Should we consider all scripture that we hear? Yes, we should, and it's for our edification. But let God's Word explain itself. Using study aids like concordances are helpful to understand how a word is being used. But most of all, let the scriptures interrupt themselves and search the references in the same context and same principles by the direction of the Holy Ghost.

God used a principle to show men how to discern; it's called "out of the mouth of two or three witnesses."

> This is the third time I am coming to you. In the mouth of two or three witnesses shall every word be established. (2 Cor. 13:1)

> One witness shall not rise up against a man for any iniquity, or for any sin, in any sin that he sin: at the mouth of two witnesses, or at the mouth of three

witnesses, shall the matter be established. (Deut. 19:15)

Moreover if thy brother shall trespass against thee, go and tell him his fault between thee and him alone: if he shall hear thee, thou hast gained thy brother. But if he will not hear thee, then take with thee one or two more, that in the mouth of two or three witnesses every word may be established. (Matt. 18:15–16)

If I bear witness of myself, my witness is not true. There is another that bears witness of me; and I know that the witness which he witness of me is true. (John 5:31–32)

Jesus spoke of the Holy Spirit of God within him, which revealed that witness. God's written Word, which Jesus spoke, is that true witness.

The helmet protects our head, and our thoughts are where we reason things out. Our reasoning should be on what God says; we should have his opinion over ours. God shows us in Scripture to have the fear [reverence] of the Lord but not to fear what sin you committed that made you "think" you lost your salvation. This is called condemnation, a feeling of judgment and having a sin conscience.

Our salvation is sealed until the day of redemption (Eph. 4:30), and we are holy to God because of Christ, not because of our worthless works, which we boast about.

Now as believers in Christ, we should walk holy in all conversation and in behavior, in good deeds and truth, being an example to win others to Christ (1 Pet. 1:15, 2 Pet. 3:11). This is a demonstration of our fellowship with God.

Jesus became our substitute to stand before God on our behalf forever. Jesus died as one of us, as a sinner (Heb. 4:15, 1 John 3:5), yet he never sinned. He was cursed so that we might be right with God. Then he freed us from the consequences of sin that brought spiritual death to present himself before God the Father on our behalf.

I can't think of any greater love or mercy that God displayed before the world through his Son.

Jesus has raised us (the church) up together in heavenly places (Eph. 1:3, 2:6, Col. 1.13 in Christ. We have access through him to have that right standing before God in holiness and acceptance. Our helmet of salvation has been sealed on top of our heads in Christ's perfect work. By no other name can you be saved (Acts 4:12). For his name indicates salvation by God.

If we fear of losing our salvation, then we are not walking in perfect love (1 John 4:18–19). We should keep our mind on what his Word says, not on ourselves. Why worry about it when you love Jesus. Just serve him and don't allow the devil to bring doubt, confusion, fear, and unbelief to draw you away from your own steadfastness.

When reading the Scriptures, you will notice the word *salvation*. It speaks at times of salvation to our spiritual soul, which is the inner man that becomes born again, and also salvation (safety soundness) concerning our behavior of our mind and heart, which directs our walk with him in fellowship.

Salvation is an example of deliverance. For example, an army winning the battle was *saved* from its enemies. Also salvation is known for healing of the body, which has been provided by the sufferings of Jesus.

It was Jesus's act that saved us, and he gave us his Holy Spirit through God. It's our privilege after we have been saved to walk with him in spirit and in truth.

To walk with him in love is when we surrender our free will over to him on a daily basis.

We make that decision every day as we listen to what God says from his written Word, either by Scripture or memory. Then we make that choice. When one surrenders, they give up the fight. We need to see it's not by our strength but by his. Jesus desires that we surrender to his will, which is his written Word, and let him live in us. And how? By us changing our mind and believing the scriptures. But it must be by a free will. He doesn't force this on us. It's God and us working together.

When we believe the truth, we receive him as Lord and Savior. Look at what happens when you do believe the truth in this passage:

> Seeing ye have purified your souls in obeying the truth through the Spirit unto unfeigned (undisguised) love of the brethren, see that ye love one another with a pure heart fervently: Being born again, not of corruptible seed, but of incorruptible, by the word of God, which live and abide for ever. For all flesh is as grass, and all the glory of man as the flower of grass. The grass wither, and the flower thereof fall away: But the word of the Lord endure for ever. And this is the word which by the gospel is preached unto you. (1 Pet. 1:22–25)

> Casting [hurl upon, cast on] all your care [distractions] upon him; for he cares [object of care] for you. Be sober, be

vigilant [awake]; because your adversary [opponent, an opponent in a suit of law an adversary, enemy] the devil, as a roaring lion, walk about, seeking whom he may devour: Whom resist steadfast in the faith, knowing that the same afflictions [also the afflictions which Christians must undergo in behalf of the same cause which Christ patiently endured] are accomplished in your brethren that are in the world. But the God of all grace, who hath called us unto his eternal glory by Christ Jesus, after that ye have suffered [experienced] a while, make you perfect, [to fit, thoroughly adjusted] established, strengthened, settle [lay a foundation, establish firmly] you. (1 Pet. 5:7–10)

God will help you make these adjustments; after all, it's God and you working together. God provided that helmet for you in the first place when you believed the truth of salvation.

And it's up to you, to not allow the devil to keep those thoughts in your mind.

Satan will try to make us think that he has knocked our helmet off our heads. Don't believe him; he is using your thoughts of fear, doubt, and confusion. *The battle is in the mind.*

That is his tactic—lying and accusing the unrenewed mind to make us feel unbalanced and uncertain of who we are in Christ and what God has already provided for us over two thousand years ago. We must renew our mind daily (Rom. 12:1–2) and speak truth that gives comfort and healing to our mind, soul, and body when we are attacked by these thoughts. By speaking, acting on the Scriptures, darkness will always flee.

And the mind will be at peace when our mind stays on him.

The Sword

Paul tells us, "And take the helmet of salvation, and the sword of the Spirit, which is the word of God."

Of all the pieces of the armor, the sword not only defends you but it is also used to destroy your enemy as you go on the offensive. It can rip into your opponent's armor. The types of armor they had in those days were either heavy cloth that was covered with leather, which the Greeks had, or heavy mail, which is made up with hundreds of small brass rings attached to one another, which one would wear over his other clothing. Also they would have brass breastplates that covered their chests. Grieves covered the lower legs. But not all the body is protected; some was exposed. Good quality of armor was very expensive and rare to the common soldier. So they would have to invest in it for better protection from their own wages. In the Roman Empire, their armor was far more protective, and it covered them throughout their body.

In combat, the soldier would try to find a way to attack an exposed area to weaken them, then they delivered the death blow.

God's sword, which is the Word of God, will weaken your enemy if you use it correctly.

Let's find some Scriptures on these battle tactics.

> For though we walk in the flesh, we do not war after the flesh: [For the weapons of our warfare are not carnal, but mighty through God to the pulling down of strong holds]; Casting down imaginations [reasonings] and every high thing that exalts [lift up or against] itself against the knowledge of God, and bringing into captivity [to take by spear] every thought to the obedience of Christ. (2 Cor. 10:3–5)

The battle ground is the mind, which is where we have victory or defeat. If our thoughts don't agree with God's written Word, then the battle is heading a different direction, not benefiting us.

By not casting down the reasonings in our mind, which exalts over his truth, We are allowing these weakened areas to affect our life. This corrupts behavior, doctrine, and the way we discern things in this world.

If it's not from the words of Jesus or from the prophets of old, through the Holy Spirit, then cast those thoughts down. Believe what God says in his Word. Don't be submissive to man's logic, reasonings, or through man's traditions or superstitions, nor their prophecies or revelations from their own wisdom.

If it's not found in God's Word, then where is the source of their information coming from? If it isn't supported by Scripture, it can't be true, and there is nothing of value. It should be rejected.

Before we came to Christ, we had these strongholds, these behaviors ruling over us. When we allow a certain sin or addiction to stay in our life, it becomes a stronghold. These shouldn't be allowed to stay as fortresses in our mind when he has given us power over it. We have the ability and authority, and we must exercise it.

When we became Christians, some of these problems departed because of the light of the truth from the Word. Those others stayed because we haven't desired for them to leave. Or we feel we don't have the strength to surrender them to Jesus just yet. Or maybe we are so bound in it, we feel it's a part of our nature, and we just accept it.

Satan can add thoughts to your mind and pluck up seeds of truth from your heart (2 Cor. 10:3–5, Heb. 2:1 Matt. 13.19, Matt. 13.25). But he can't enter into your spiritually sealed soul (Eph. 4:30), which is your holy of holies, where God's spirit resides.

But devils can enter into the flesh because of sin and add thoughts to our mind to corrupt our heart. But by God's Word, confessing, agreeing, believing and acting on it will cause the devil to flee. This isn't by our strength or our human power. It's by his Spirit and his strength, giving over our will to his. It's making a decision each day. Are we going to walk in the spirit or the flesh? (Gal. 5:16).

Light will always chase out darkness, and when we draw near to God by his Word and through meditation of his promises, by casting down these thoughts and relying on his Word, that's when Satan will flee.

God's Word is like water; its cleansing water will free your mind and cleanse your bodies because it's not by your power but the power he has given us through his Holy Spirit and the words he spoke to mortal man.

You can seek counselors, friends, and anyone that you can think of, and it might help at times. But truly only living in the spirit, we will overcome the desires of the flesh. That is what's going to free us from our addictions, knowing that God loves us and resting and believing on what he says from the written Word. He knows what you are going through and with good instruction, will show you how to be free from it by his written Word.

But we have a free will, and we must have a desire to do so, believing, acting, trusting, and resting in his Word. Only then will you see the promises of deliverance. All things are possible to him that believes (Mark 9:23).

Plus, don't have fellowship with the things that are causing that temptation. If you have a problem with drinking, don't socialize with others who like to drink because it's going to tempt you more. It's that simple.

We are at war with the devil, and yes, Jesus won that war over two thousand years ago. But as you notice, we still have to fight the good fight of faith as long as we are here on this earth. And by the way, you're going to win through God if you're agreeing in obedience on what he says from his Word as he trains you.

These battles will continue until we see him, for we are still mortals.

> But I fear, lest by any means, as the serpent beguiled [deceived] Eve through his subtilty [cunning], so your minds should be corrupted from the simplicity that is in Christ.
>
> For if he that cometh preach another Jesus, whom we have not preached, or if ye receive another spirit, which ye have not received, or another gospel, which ye have not accepted, ye might well bear with him. (2 Cor. 11:3–4)

If you read 1 Corinthians 1, Paul wrote this to Christians. He understood how the devil was dividing the church. Paul stated in 2 Corinthians 11 that he feared that just as Eve was deceived by Satan's seduction, your minds could be corrupted from the simplicity that is in Christ.

Paul continues later in 2 Corinthians.

> For such are false apostles, deceitful workers, transforming themselves into the apostles of Christ. And no marvel;

for Satan himself is transformed into an angel of light. Therefore it is no great thing if his ministers also be transformed as the ministers of righteousness; whose end shall be according to their works. (2 Cor. 11:13–15)

Paul also made it perfectly clear that if one came speaking about another Jesus, which means *savior* in Greek, which they didn't preach, or if they receive another spirit or another gospel that you have not accepted, you might bear with him, that does these things.

Paul is warning the church in love, "Don't be led away from the truth by other false saviors, spirits, and teachings apart from the scriptures and the words of Jesus (Yahshua) himself."

It would bless us if we would read these books, 1 Corinthians and 2 Corinthians to see what Paul taught the Church.

Let's continue.

> Let this mind be in you, which was also in Christ Jesus: Who, being in the form of God, thought it not robbery to be equal with God: But made himself of no reputation, and took upon him the form of a servant, and was made in the likeness of men: And being found in fashion as a man, he humbled himself, and became obedient unto death, even the death of the cross. Wherefore God also hath highly exalted him, and given him a name which is above every name: That at the name of Jesus every knee should bow, of things in heaven, and things in earth, and things under the earth. (Phil. 2:5–10)

Paul tells us where our mind should be, just as Jesus's mind was on God. We should be watchful of our own thoughts. We must not try to develop a worldly reputation. Let's humble ourselves to God's Word. Let's be aware of what we hear and where it's coming from, knowing that Satan will try to seduce us in any way through his cunningness and tactics of the world. Satan will try to confuse us and bring doubt to the simplicity (lack of complication) that is in Christ.

> Study to show thyself approved [tested and tried] unto God, a workman that need not to be ashamed, rightly dividing the word of truth. But shun profane and vain babblings: for they will increase unto more ungodliness. (2 Tim. 2:15–16)

> Beloved, believe not every spirit, but try the spirits whether they are of God: because many false prophets are gone out into the world. Hereby know ye the Spirit of God: Every spirit that confesses that Jesus Christ is come in the flesh is of God: And every spirit that confesses not that Jesus Christ is come in the flesh is not of God: and this is that spirit of antichrist, whereof ye have heard that it should come; and even now already is it in the world. They are of the world:

therefore they speak of the world, and the world hears them. (1 John 4:1–3, 5)

This gives us a clue of what spirit they are of; they speak of the world and the world hears them. Jesus tells us the world didn't receive him, and if we walk with him, they will not receive us.

I have given them thy word; and the world hath hated them, because they are not of the world, even as I am not of the world. I pray not that thou should take them out of the world, but that thou should keep them from the evil. They are not of the world, even as I am not of the world. (John 17:14–16)

A careful study of this chapter will give more understanding of what John wrote.

This below displays an awesome example of the written Word of God in action.

For the word of God is quick [alive] and powerful [energetic] and sharper [acute, more cutting] than any two-edged sword, piercing [come through] even to the dividing asunder of soul and spirit, and of the joints and marrow, and is a discerner [critic judge] of the thoughts and intents of the heart. Neither is there any creature that is not manifest in his sight: but all things are naked and opened unto the eyes of him with whom we have to do. Seeing then that we have a great high priest, that is passed into the heavens, Jesus the Son of God, let us hold fast our profession. For we have not an high priest which cannot be touched with the feeling of our infirmities; but was in all points tempted like as we are, yet without sin. Let us therefore come boldly unto the throne of grace, that we may obtain mercy, and find grace to help in time of need. (Heb. 4:12–16)

Let's cover this point: "even to the dividing asunder of soul and spirit, and of the joints and marrow, and is a discerner of the thoughts and intents of the heart."

God's Word will divide or reveal if we are saved or not. It will reveal if we have the spirit of God (being born again) in our spiritual soul or not. We have a choice either to receive Jesus as Lord and Savior, which will allow the spirit of God to enter into our soul for eternal life or to reject it and be judged by the Word without Christ, to be sentenced to eternal destruction. God's Word is the critic and judge on what is truth and error. God's Word shows us if we have Christ's Spirit or not (Rom. 8:9).

Also God's Word benefits our body for healing the joints and marrow. And to our mind, sound health.

> My son, forget not my law; but let thine heart keep my commandments: For length of days, and long life, and peace, shall they add to thee. Let not mercy [kindness, loving-kindness] and truth forsake thee: bind them about thy neck;

write them upon the table of thine heart: So shall thou find favour [grace] and good understanding in the sight of God and man. Trust in the Lord with all thine heart; and lean not unto thine own understanding. In all thy ways acknowledge him, and he shall direct thy paths. Be not wise in thine own eyes: fear the Lord, and depart from evil. It shall be health to thy navel, and marrow to thy bones. (Prov. 3:1–8)

God's Word will heal your nerves (marrow, from Hebrew) and your bones. As a matter of fact, God promises from his Word that he will heal your whole body. Either you can believe this or not. You can stay sick in mind and in body or be healed. But that doesn't change God's promises to those who believe he is able.

God's Word will judge or discern our thoughts and our intentions. Below are a few examples.

> O generation of vipers, how can ye, being evil, speak good things? for out of the abundance of the heart the mouth speak. A good man out of the good treasure of the heart bring forth good things: and an evil man out of the evil treasure bring forth evil things. (Matt. 12:34–35)

> A good man out of the good treasure of his heart bring forth that which is good; and an evil man out of the evil treasure of his heart bring forth that which is evil: for of the abundance of the heart his mouth speak. (Luke 6:45)

Our heart will reveal our thoughts and our intentions, so it's important that we speak good things, and nothing is better than the life-giving Word of God, which brings life.

> I beseech you therefore, brethren, by the mercies of God, that ye present your bodies a living sacrifice, holy, acceptable [well pleasing] unto God, which is your reasonable service. And be not conformed

to this world: but be ye transformed by the renewing of your mind [will] that ye may prove what is that good, and acceptable, and perfect [ended, complete] will of God. (Rom. 12:1–2)

When we renew our mind by studying his Word, we learn his thoughts through his Word, which is the sword of the spirit. We also learn through the testimonies of all those who faced different challenges in the Bible. Some had the victory, and some fell into failure, but nevertheless, they became witnesses to us as examples of making right and wrong decisions.

God's Word, the Sword, can be used wrongly and ignorantly. It should not be used to hack on the person we are talking to or being in the wrong spirit with twisted doctrines and manipulation to control others.

God's Word thrusts into the mind and into the heart of the conscience of the soul to bring conviction not condemnation, shame, or guilt. His Word is peaceful and restful. But it does correct and instruct us, and if we are not willing to receive it, we can feel that it judges us and pokes at what we believe or think. But at the same time, it builds us up in truth and encourages us.

God wants us to renew our mind daily by his Word; he doesn't want us to be ruled by our fleshly emotions, and he wants us to rule over them, not for them to rule over us. Turn it over to God by reading his written Word, by praying, and by being thankful. Satan will always tell us that it's a personal attack on you when someone shares with you. It doesn't hurt to hear and to take careful consideration.

This displays spiritual maturity and our responsibility. It isn't a personal attack when we understand; our body is God's temple, and we don't belong to ourselves. So why defend this old body of sin when we can live and walk in the spirit?

Let's allow his wondrous Scriptures to encourage us, give us peace, build us up, bring us courage and confidence to uncover truth and error, and give us wisdom from his love toward us who believe. God wants us to understand who we are in Christ, as born-again believers.

Once we understand this, then nothing will cause us to stumble if we rest, trust, giving every problem to him, and knowing it's to our advantage, for he loves us.

> And beside this, giving all diligence, add to your faith virtue; and to virtue knowledge; And to knowledge temperance [self-control]; and to temperance patience; and to patience godliness; And to godliness brotherly kindness; and to brotherly kindness charity. For if these things be in you, and abound [to make more], they make you that ye shall neither be barren [empty] nor unfruitful [without fruit] in the knowledge of our Lord Jesus Christ. But he that lack [not to be near one]

these things is blind, and cannot see afar off, and hath forgotten that he was purged from his old sins. Wherefore the rather, brethren, give diligence to make your calling and election sure: for if ye do these things, ye shall never fall [stumble] For so an entrance [a way in] shall be ministered unto you abundantly into the everlasting kingdom of our Lord and Saviour Jesus Christ. (2 Pet. 1:5–11)

God wants that fullness in you; it's through his knowledge that we have understanding of grace and peace in our minds and hearts (1 Peter 1:2). Please read this whole chapter; it will bless you.

In 1 Corinthians 2:14–15, it reads, "But the natural man receives not the things of the Spirit of God: for they are foolishness unto him: neither can he know them, because they are spiritually discerned. But he that is spiritual judge all things, yet he himself is judged of no man."

Paul writes about the carnal man, or the natural man. Also he describes the spiritual man. Paul writes that a spiritual man judges or discerns all things, and the natural man doesn't receive the things of God, because it's foolish to him, he isn't discerning between truth or error. The natural man doesn't accept God's Word as the final authority. The spiritual man is a person who is first saved then walking in the truth, through what God's servants are sharing from the scriptures (Old Testament), the gospels, and epistles in the New Testament.

God's Word provides discernment on what is true or false and what spirit is speaking to us through that doctrine. This is the reason why we should judge all things but not people.

"Judge the doctrine and the spirit carrying the message by God's Word. Don't judge on the outward appearance" (John 7:24).

> But God hath revealed them unto us by his Spirit: for the Spirit search all things, yea, the deep things of God. For what

man knows the things of a man, save the spirit of man which is in him? even so the things of God knows no man, but the Spirit of God. Now we have received, not the spirit of the world, but the spirit which is of God; that we might know the things that are freely given to us of God. Which things also we speak, not in the words which man's wisdom teaches, but which the Holy Ghost teaches; comparing spiritual things with spiritual. But the natural [natural, sensual] man receives not the things of the Spirit of God: for they are foolishness unto him: neither can he know them, because they are spiritually discerned [examine, judge closely]. But he that is spiritual, judges all things, yet he himself is judged of no man. For who hath known the mind of the Lord, that he may instruct him? but we have the mind of Christ. (1 Cor. 2:10–16)

The spiritual man waits on God, discerns all things, prays, and searches the Scriptures for the answer. He doesn't believe every spirit, dream, vision, or prophecy. And he isn't ruled by feelings and emotions. He forgives everyone and prays for them in a right heart. He isn't led by his sense knowledge but by the written Word.

He is calm, peaceful, and settled in his mind on what the Scripture says. Plus the fruit of the spirit just continues to increase in him every day. He is like a watered garden (Isa. 58:11). A born-again, saved believer can become carnally minded, and we often do. We lose our cool and get angry, but we shouldn't let our anger go down with the sun; we let it go (Eph. 4:26), and at times, our fruit of the spirit could have fewer worms in it and also less dark spots or blemishes. But we can renew our thoughts daily by his Word and learn to change our behavior with God's Word to increase our growth in him. It's up to us, and we are fully aware that God wants to work with us and in us.

The sword of the spirit is something we use every day. Satan doesn't rest. But we rest in the truth because of the weapons that God has provided, which is his written Word. In the book of Revelations, it reveals the power of the sword. Notice this:

> And out of his mouth goeth a sharp sword, that with it he should smite the nations: and he shall rule them with a rod of iron: and he treadeth the winepress of the fierceness and wrath of Almighty God. (Rev. 19:15)

This sword is the *written Word* that he speaks. Also notice in the book of Matthew.

> When the even was come, they brought unto him many that were possessed with devils: and he cast out the spirits with his word, and healed all that were sick:
>
> That it might be fulfilled which was spoken by Esaias the prophet, saying,

Himself took our infirmities, and bare our sicknesses. (Matt. 8:16–17)

As you notice, Jesus cast out the spirits with his Word. And he has provided this power to the church, if we believe. The *sword is the Word of God.* You have the same power as Jesus did, for he is within you. And he wants us to speak his Word and watch him work. He gave power to the twelve disciples, then another seventy people who believed, to send them forth to preach (Luke 9:1–2, Luke 9:49–50, Luke 10:1–21). And more was added to the church after his resurrection (Acts 1:15, Acts 2:41). We believed when we heard the *Word of Truth.* But do we understand all the benefits we have from him, through the Holy Ghost? If we are willing, God will reveal it in the scriptures.

Pray Always

> Praying always with all prayer and supplication in the Spirit, and watching thereunto with all perseverance and supplication for all saints.
>
> —Ephesians 6:18

What is prayer? From this Greek word *proseuchē*, it means prayer or a pouring out, prayer addressed to God. Here are a few scriptures from this same Greek word to show how it's used in context.

> Let love be without dissimulation [not hypocritical or as an actor]. Abhor [shrink from] that which is evil; cleave to that which is good. Be kindly affection [loving with natural affection] one to another with brotherly love; in honor preferring [to lend before] one another; Not slothful [not motionless, or lazy] in business; fervent [hot to boil] in spirit; serving

the Lord; Rejoicing in hope; patient in tribulation [pressure]; continuing instant in prayer [prayer pouring out]; Distributing to the necessity of saints; given to hospitality [a love of strangers]. Bless them which persecute you: bless, and curse not. Rejoice with them that do rejoice, and weep with them that weep. Be of the same mind one toward another. Mind not high things, but condescend to men of low estate [humble]. Be not wise in your own conceits. Recompense [give away back fully] to no man evil for evil. Provide things honest in the sight of all men. Dearly beloved, avenge not yourselves, but rather give place unto wrath: for it is written, Vengeance is mine; I will repay, saith the Lord.

Therefore if thine enemy hunger, feed him; if he thirst, give him drink: for in so doing thou shalt heap coals of fire on his head. Be not overcome of evil, but overcome evil with good. (Rom. 12:9–21)

Be careful [distracted] for nothing; but in every thing by prayer and supplication [deprecation] with thanksgiving let your requests be made known unto God. And the peace of God, which pass all understanding, shall keep [guard] your hearts and minds through Christ Jesus.

Finally, brethren, whatsoever things are true, whatsoever things are honest, whatsoever things are just, whatsoever things are pure, whatsoever things are lovely, whatsoever things are of good report; if there be any virtue, and if there be any praise, think on these things. Those things, which ye have both learned, and received, and heard, and seen in me, do: and the God of peace shall be with you. (Phil. 4:6–9)

The word *deprecation* in the dictionary means "to avert by prayer." To avert means to turn aside or away. Avert the eyes so that you're not allowing your natural senses; to focus on the problem, but by pouring out your requests to the

Lord, seeking his advice by faith in his promises from his written will.

This next scripture directs the importance to pray for our loved ones and each other as we are one body in Christ.

> Likewise, ye husbands, dwell with them according to knowledge, giving honor unto the wife, as unto the weaker vessel, and as being heirs together of the grace of life; that your prayers be not hindered. Finally, be ye all of one mind, having compassion [suffering or feeling the like with another], one of another, love as brethren, be pitiful, [tenderhearted, compassionate], be courteous [friendly, kind]. Not rendering evil for evil, or railing for railing [speaking reproachfully]: but contrariwise blessing; knowing that ye are thereunto called, that ye should inherit a blessing. For he that will love life, and see good days, let him refrain his tongue from evil, and his lips that they speak no guile

[craft, deceit]. Let him eschew [bend out] evil, and do good; let him seek peace, and ensue [pursue, run after] it.

For the eyes of the Lord are over the righteous, and his ears are open unto their prayers: but the face of the Lord is against them that do evil. And who is he that will harm you, if ye be followers of that which is good? But and if ye suffer for righteousness' sake, happy are ye: and be not afraid of their terror, neither be troubled; But sanctify the Lord God in your hearts: and be ready always to give an answer to every man that asketh you a reason of the hope that is in you with meekness and fear: Having a good conscience; that, whereas they speak evil of you, as of evildoers, they may be ashamed that falsely accuse your good conversation [behavior, conduct] in Christ. For it is better, if the will of God be so, that ye suffer for well doing, than for evil doing. (1 Pet. 3:7–17)

God wants you to pray for others that you don't know, to receive salvation. And for believers in Christ to have wisdom, knowledge, and guidance by his Word. God also wants you to pray for everything in your life. Pray about all things that you do. Do all in the name of Jesus Christ in word and in deed. Seek his advice and wisdom; he will teach you.

As a requirement of our prayers, do it with perseverance (firmness of mind) and supplication (a seeking, asking, entreating, request) for all saints. Be firm on what God's written Word speaks to us. Let that peace surround you, and let it be your comfort.

> Confess your faults one to another, and pray one for another, that ye may be healed. The effectual fervent prayer of a righteous man avails much. (James 5:16)

Know who you are in Christ and humbly give all glory and thankfulness to him every day in your life while you are here in this world. Pray always, and seek God's wisdom, which he will give when we ask him.

Improving and Strengthening Your Armor

During the Roman empire, the soldier had to maintain his own armor, keep it clean, fix the dents, and repair it where needed. Because of the long campaigns, the armor was affected by weather—rain, dust and cold resulted in rust, plus engagements over the years against the enemy would take its toll. These soldiers understood the importance of their armor. It was a matter of life and death if they didn't repair their armor. When they had the time, they would put attention toward their armor to make sure it was strong and ready for any battle.

As believers in Christ, we should do the same with our *spiritual armor*—keeping our helmet on tight, shield high and strong, and our sword sharp. We exercise our mind on all the pieces of the *armor that God* has provided and its purpose (1 Tim. 4:7–8).

As you grow in your Christian walk, your prayer life, knowledge, and wisdom will also increase which the Lord gives by his written Word. God wants you to be confident and bold, being assured of your salvation, which is complete in him. The accuser, which is Satan, will use anything and anyone to bring doubt, which will increase confusion. This will bring instability and fear if we allow it. This is the wrong type of fear to have. God desires that we fear (reverence) his Word, and his Word will strengthen us and improve our walk with Christ.

Each day should start being thankful and being mindful of who we are in Christ, which can bring a song in our heart. Remember a scripture that will encourage and remind us of God's grace. Speak good things, and let your mind be clean and fresh with his Word. Spend a little time with the Lord every day with prayer and his written Word. Make that your *Sabbath* every day, and rest in his promises in the Scriptures. It doesn't depend on how much you read, but what you learn from it. We need to clothe our mind daily of who we are in Christ and not to remind ourselves of the negative things that this world will bring.

We should have a good confession, watch our words, and harness our tongue. Keeping it contained in our thoughts of what we were and who we are now in Christ, a New Creature. Let these scriptures below bless you.

> But now ye also put off all these; anger, wrath, malice, blasphemy, filthy communication out of your mouth. Lie not one to another, seeing that ye have put off the old man with his deeds; And have put on the new man, which is renewed in knowledge after the image of him that created him: Where there is neither Greek nor Jew, circumcision nor uncircumcision, Barbarian, Scythian, bond nor free: but Christ is all, and in all. Put on therefore, as

the elect of God, holy and beloved, bowels of mercies, kindness, humbleness of mind, meekness, longsuffering; Forbearing [to hold back self] one another, and forgiving one another, if any man have a quarrel against any: even as Christ forgave you, so also do ye. And above all these things put on charity, which is the bond of perfectness. And let the peace of God rule in your hearts, to the which also ye are called in one body; and be ye thankful. Let the word of Christ dwell in you richly in all wisdom; teaching and admonishing [to put into the mind] one another in psalms and hymns and spiritual songs, singing with grace in your hearts to the Lord. And whatsoever ye do in word or deed, do all in the name of the Lord Jesus, giving thanks to God and the Father by him. (Col. 3:8–17)

That ye put off [unclothe] concerning the former conversation [behavior] the old man, which is corrupt according to the deceitful lusts; And be renewed in the spirit of your mind [will]; And that ye put on the new man, which after God is created in righteousness and true holiness. Wherefore putting away lying, speak every man truth with his neighbour: for we are members one of another. Be ye angry, and sin not: let not the sun go down upon your wrath: Neither give [spot, room] place to the devil. Let him that stole steal no more: but rather let him labor, working with his hands the thing which is good, that he may have to give to him that need. Let no corrupt communication proceed out of your mouth, but that which is good to the use of edifying [building up], that it may minister grace unto the hearers. And grieve not the Holy Spirit of God, whereby ye are sealed unto the day of redemption. Let all bitterness, and wrath, and anger, and clamour [a crying, outcry] and evil speaking, be put away from you, with all malice: And be ye kind one to another,

tenderhearted [compassionate] forgiving
one another, even as God for Christ's sake
hath forgiven you. (Eph. 4:22–32)

Don't allow the devil to have room in your life.
That room starts in your thought life. God wants
you to put forth this effort of believing who you
are in Christ from the beginning to the end.

Here is something to think about. Does God
physically dress you in the morning or yourself?
It's just that simple, having a desire to change
once you become his child and starting a new
life with him, walking with him in fellowship.
Bring down those strongholds in your mind and
those bad habits that you had before. Do not
listen to those thoughts but rely on his written
Word and cast down those thoughts. If you
believe you can't change, you won't change. It's
your decision, and God will strengthen you.

For as he think in his heart, so is he: Eat
and drink, saith he to thee; but his heart
is not with thee. (Prov. 23:7)

134

Apply your heart unto instruction, and your ears to the words of knowledge. (Prov. 23:12)

As you study, read, pray and meditate on what you have learned, this will build your armor. Plus having experience by tribulation and pressure in this world will improve your armor. Place your trust in his Word when things look difficult. And believe his promises from the scriptures.

Let them now that fear the Lord say, that his mercy endures for ever. I called upon the Lord in distress: the Lord answered me, and set me in a large place. The Lord is on my side; I will not fear: what can man do unto me? The Lord take my part with them that help me: therefore shall I see my desire upon them that hate me. It is better to trust in the Lord than to put confidence in man. It is better to trust in the Lord than to put confidence in princes. (Ps. 118:4–9)

For the Lord shall be thy confidence [firmness], and shall keep thy foot from being taken. (Prov. 3:26)

In the fear of the Lord is strong confidence: and his children shall have a place of refuge. (Prov. 14: 26)

And this is the confidence that we have in him, that, if we ask any thing according to his will, he hears us: And if we know that he hear us, whatsoever we ask, we know that we have the petitions that we desired of him. (1 John 5:14–15)

My little children, let us not love in word, neither in tongue; but in deed and in truth. And hereby we know that we are of the truth, and shall assure our hearts before him. For if our heart condemn us, God is greater than our heart, and knoweth all things. Beloved, if our heart condemn us not, then have we confidence toward God. And whatsoever we ask, we receive of him, because we keep his commandments, and do those things that are pleasing in his sight. And this is his commandment, That we should believe on the name of his Son Jesus Christ, and love one another, as he gave us commandment. And he that keepeth his commandments dwelleth in him, and he in him. And hereby we know that he abideth in us, by the Spirit which he hath given us. (1 John 3:18–24)

Let's go over a few points on what we discussed.

God wants you to be strong in the Lord and in his power (Eph. 6:10).

God wants us to put on the whole armor. He wants you to know every part of his armor and how to use it, not just giving attention to certain parts of it (Eph 6: 11).

God wants you to be aware of your enemy, the devil (Eph. 6:12, 1 Pet. 5:8).

God wants you to know his character or nature, his righteousness, his mercy, his judgment, his love toward you, and his full dedication to you as your captain, who shall train you for battle (Eph. 4:1–32, Eph. 6:10–13, Heb. 4.11–14).

God wants you to meditate, read, and study his Word (Joshua 1:8, 2 Tim. 2:15). This will reveal truth and error, sin and righteousness.

God wants you to apply his principles from his Word into your walk (Col. 1:9–13, 2:6–10).

God wants you to know that you will suffer the same persecutions as his Son did on the earth when you share the truth.

> These things I have spoken unto you, that in me ye might have peace. In the world ye shall have tribulation: but be of good cheer; I have overcome [gain the victory] the world. (John 16.33)

> Therefore I take pleasure in infirmities, in reproaches, in necessities, in persecutions, in distresses for Christ's sake: for when I am weak, then am I strong. (2 Cor. 12:10)

> So that we ourselves glory in you in the churches of God for your patience

and faith in all your persecutions and tribulations that ye endure. (2 Thess. 1:4)

Yea, and all that will live godly in Christ Jesus shall suffer persecution. (2 Tim. 3:12)

Our Lord took all our sickness and sins and paid the price for the wages of sin (Isa. 53:3–6). But we shall suffer as Christians in this world (Phil. 1:27–29). If the world didn't like what Jesus said, they will not like what you say if you are speaking his words, you will be rejected. (Rom. 8:17, 1 Tim. 4:10, 1 Pet. 4:16).

We don't praise God for the hole we fell in, but we praise God for the deliverance.

This world doesn't like you, so don't try to seek for its acceptance. Be a good example in faith, love, conversation, and deeds. But don't deny the Word that is in your heart.

Christians in *this world* will always be looked down upon as fools. They see us as ignorant, not binding to conformity in culture, and out of step.

If we speak the same things that Jesus spoke, we will receive the same type of treatment.

But we can make a difference in this world. Share your testimony in Christ and speak God's Word in love and boldness in the Holy Ghost. Share the full gospel. Then let God deal with them. Look at our example, the apostle Paul, who wrote in the spirit.

> For Christ sent me not to baptize, but to preach the gospel: not with wisdom of words, lest the cross of Christ should be made of none effect. For the preaching of the cross is to them that perish foolishness; but unto us which are saved it is the power of God. For it is written, I will destroy the wisdom of the wise, and will bring to nothing the understanding of the prudent. Where is the wise? where is the scribe? where is the disputer of this world? hath not God made foolish the wisdom of this world? For after that in the wisdom of God the world by wisdom

knew not God, it pleased God by the foolishness of preaching to save them that believe. For the Jews require a sign, and the Greeks seek after wisdom: But we preach Christ crucified, unto the Jews a stumblingblock, and unto the Greeks foolishness; But unto them which are called, both Jews and Greeks, Christ the power of God, and the wisdom of God. Because the foolishness of God is wiser than men; and the weakness of God is stronger than men. For ye see your calling, brethren, how that not many wise men after the flesh, not many mighty, not many noble, are called: But God hath chosen the foolish things of the world to confound the wise; and God hath chosen the weak things of the world to confound the things which are mighty; And base things of the world, and things which are despised, hath God chosen, yea, and things which are not, to bring to nought things that are: That no flesh

> should glory in his presence. But of him
> are ye in Christ Jesus, who of God is
> made unto us wisdom, and righteousness,
> and sanctification, and redemption: That,
> according as it is written, He that glories,
> let him glory in the Lord. (1 Cor. 1:17–31)

If they hate or oppose Jesus's words, they will not approve of you if you are speaking the same things as did he.

God wants you to be holy in conversation and deeds since you are already holy through the sacrifice that Jesus went through. God wants you to pray or pour out your heart to him, talking to your Heavenly Father daily in the name of Jesus.

God wants you to know that Satan is conquered and Jesus spoiled and defeated the enemy, yet Satan doesn't think so, and he will challenge us daily on the battlefield in our mind. Be ready to fight. Be ready to stand firm. Have confidence and courage; God will not let you fall. Trust and receive his words.

God wants you to know you are a conqueror; you have the victory and can do all things through Christ Jesus. You can study his Word to rest your thoughts from every care and worry.

Worry is nothing but overflowing waves from the ocean of fear. But by having a strong, confident mind, believing in his promises that God is able, you will stand against those waves; you will be on the high rock of truth. Remember how Jesus calmed the storm with his words? It's the same action we should take. When we cast down these negative thoughts and replace them with the promises in his written Word, we will see a big difference. There will be peace and calm in our lives.

Believe that the Lord will help you in any storm, and claim it as victory.

Also we need to give thanks every day, in song, prayer, conversation, and a good confession by his Word. Singing with all your heart will remind you what he did for you and what is in store for you in the future. Thankfulness is also a part of prayer. Repentance is just changing our mind to what God wrote down in scripture and believing him.

When we renew and change our mind by letting his Holy Scriptures instruct us, it will change our behavior, and it produces fruit of gratitude.

> Neither filthiness, nor foolish talking, nor jesting, which are not convenient: but rather giving of thanks. (Eph. 5:4)

> But thanks be to God, which gives us the victory through our Lord Jesus Christ. (1 Cor. 15:57)

> And whatsoever ye do in word or deed, do all in the name of the Lord Jesus, giving thanks to God and the Father by him. (Col. 3:17)

> Wherefore be ye not unwise, but understanding what the will of the Lord is. And be not drunk with wine, wherein is excess; but be filled with the Spirit;

Speaking to yourselves in psalms and hymns and spiritual songs, singing and making melody in your heart to the Lord; Giving thanks always for all things unto God and the Father in the name of our Lord Jesus Christ; Submitting yourselves one to another in the fear of God. (Eph. 5:17–21)

If you see this as legalism, studying and reading his Word or any performance of good works encouraged by his apostles and disciples, then you are reasoning and trying to justify it within yourselves, "listening to another spirit".

Why worry about it? Just serve the Lord, and do it in joy and in his peace. Don't let anyone rob from you your joy in obeying and receiving his written Word. Don't let the devil rob from you your peace.

There are many scriptures on this; as we study, God will show us.

THE INHERITANCE
OF THE SAINTS

It is so important to understand how God sees us in him and how it will affect our prayer life. God has provided many benefits to assist us while we are here on earth. Jesus said he wouldn't leave us or forsake us. So I must admit that believing what he says should have full authority over all what we feel or think.

As we read his Word, this inheritance becomes more tangible than we first realized. If only we look more into it as looking for hidden treasures.

If we believe what Scripture says, then we will see the power from his words.

Let's cover some of these benefits from the Lord. Let's discover this together. If you already have, praise the Lord. Continue in it. Believe and remember the goodness of the Lord.

No weapon that is formed against thee shall prosper; and every tongue that shall rise against thee in judgment thou shall condemn [to make or declare wrong in law]. This is the heritage of the servants of the Lord, and their righteousness is of me, say's the Lord. (Isa. 54:17)

We can believe this or we can try to reason this out with our own understanding. But nevertheless, God spoke this, and either God is speaking truth or he's lying. And God said he does not lie (Num. 23:19).

If you ever wanted a rich relative, well, you have one: when you came into the family of God. It just can't get any better. Man has studied, endeavored, and labored to be rich in this world, and what has it brought him? Stress and fear of losing that money he worked so hard to obtain. He has endured competition, which produces the fruit of envy, strife, hatred, worry, stress, which brings ill health plus instability in many other ways. Mankind is always trying to fill that need that money can't buy, which can never be satisfied.

But there is good news: this need can be filled by God's Spirit, giving life and fulfillment, which brings peace. It only comes by receiving Christ Jesus as Lord and Savior.

When someone receives an inheritance from a family member who passed away, they can become suspicious and fearful with their money, worrying that they might be taken advantage of. So they become tighter, hanging on to it.

Is it wrong to be rich? Is it wrong to be poor? Both situations can cause you problems.

Look at this scripture.

> Remove far from me vanity and lies: give me neither poverty nor riches; feed me with food convenient [limited and apportioned] for me: Lest I be full, and deny thee, and say, Who is the Lord? or lest I be poor, and steal, and take the name of my God in vain. (Prov. 30:8–9)

This really sums it up. Is money the root of all evil? No, but the desire or love for it is the trap. This is Satan's trap.

God wants you to be responsible for your own life's decisions, and he will work with you if you are willing. He can't and won't do it alone. You both must work together by faith.

Look at what Paul wrote to Timothy concerning gain.

> Perverse disputings of men of corrupt minds, and destitute of the truth, supposing that gain is godliness: from such withdraw thyself. But godliness with contentment [self-sufficient] is great gain. For we brought nothing into this world, and it is certain we can carry nothing out. And having food and raiment let us be therewith content. But they that will be rich fall into temptation and a snare [fastening net], and into many foolish and hurtful lusts, which drown [sink] men in destruction and perdition. For the love

[Greek word philargyria: to be a friend or avarice] of money is the root of all evil: which while some coveted after, they have erred from the faith, and pierced themselves through with many sorrows. But thou, O man of God, flee these things; and follow after righteousness, godliness, faith, love, patience, meekness. (1 Tim. 6:5–11)

God teaches us to be content with what we have, and his Word will reveal to us what we should truly desire and what we should reflect in our behavior.

The true inheritance that we have in Jesus Christ is putting on the whole armor of God, and we should wear it every day.

Don't worry or be anxious; remember the birds? (Matt. 6:26). God makes sure he feeds them. Aren't we more valuable than them? He will have compassion on those that reverence him and love him. It's his desire that you learn his will, and his will comes by understanding his written Word.

If we read and study God's Word every day, what riches can we discover? What mysteries and frontiers can we imagine? What knowledge will be opened up to us? God's Word has power if you believe.

It will free and change our minds if we allow it. It will develop good behavior and our actions toward one another. We at times will fall and stumble, but he will lift us up by the encouragement from his Word. We can pray, sing, and give our will over to him. For he knows us better than we know ourselves.

God's Word will train our mind, heart, and tongue on how to speak and what to speak. It will show us the difference of truth and error, of sin, righteousness, and judgment. It will reveal the name of Jesus and the benefits that go with it. Most of all, it will bring knowledge of salvation that rescues us from the bottomless pit if we accept him as Lord and Savior.

Can we ever be so grateful and thankful of all that he has provided? Can we ever find the words to show God how much we appreciate all that he has done? I can't think of one. Instead, let's show our gratitude through obedience; let's show that we love him by walking with him starting today.

Focusing on the Invisible

Because we live in a visual world, it only seems normal and natural to keep our eyes on what we see. We gaze upon the world in wonder, the mountains, valleys, rivers, and seas. We wonder in amazement upon the formations of the splendor of creation all around us. We awake from a deep sleep and go about our daily chores to make a living. We plan, live, and explore what we desire in this mortal body. At times we struggle, complain, and bicker because of the events that come across our way. But we feel relieved when we come home to an atmosphere of rest and comfort.

We are people of habit, someone once said. We at times just don't think about things that don't physically relate to us. Remember that old saying? "I'll believe it when I see it." If we feel it has no purpose or value in our daily reasoning and logic, then we have no use for it.

We know God is a Spirit (John 4:24). We know that we can't see him with our eyes. It's the same with the wind. You can't see it, but you can see what it does (John 3:7–8). We can feel the wind and experience its power toward us and our surroundings. But we can't physically see it.

We believe in God by faith, and we have faith by hearing or reading his Word. Then when we perform what he says, we can see how he works and experience that spiritual wind. It moves the hearts, changes minds, and brings in peace that the world can never supply, and it makes the impossible become possible.

If God lives and performs all things by faith, shouldn't we?

Look at what the writer said.

> Now faith [steadfastness] is the substance of things hoped for, the evidence of things not seen. For by it the elders obtained a

good report. Through faith we understand that the worlds were framed by the word of God, so that things which are seen were not made of things which do appear. (Heb. 11:1–3)

God spoke these things, and it came into existence. He knew his words would form everything that he wanted. That is steadfastness. Now, we know we are not God, but he has given his Spirit to the church and he made us children of God. What we need to understand is to look through his eyes to see things as they are, and the only way is knowing what his prophets wrote down.

The problem is we at times don't believe his words and don't pay attention to the invisible, thinking it's just a figment of our imagination or to comfort ourselves by words we read in a book. The Bible is more than a book; it's a gathering of books of testimonies from men and woman who learned there is a God in heaven and his Son that was promised, "from the foundation of the world" (Rev. 13:8) is the only way to God.

We have a choice to either believe it or not. God isn't going to force you to believe. But the question is, do these things exist? Is it a fantasy or illusion?

If we believe in God, then there are angels and devils—which are unclean spirits—and of course, Satan himself. If we are born-again Christians, we most definitely should pay more attention to the things invisible. Here are some scriptures that give us wisdom and knowledge from those who experienced the invisible.

In 2 Kings 6, we have the king of Syria that was going to make war with Israel. But God had Elisha to stand for Israel.

Note the events as we read.

> Therefore sent he thither horses, and chariots, and a great host: and they came by night, and compassed the city about.

And when the servant of the man of God was risen early, and gone forth, behold, an host compassed the city both with horses and chariots. And his servant said unto him, Alas, my master! how shall we do? And he answered, Fear not: for they that be with us are more than they that be with them. And Elisha prayed, and said, Lord, I pray thee, open his eyes, that he may see. And the Lord opened the eyes of the young man; and he saw: and, behold, the mountain was full of horses and chariots of fire round about Elisha. (2 Kings 6:14–17)

Elisha saw the army of the Lord by faith, and when he prayed, God revealed the invisible. God had a supernatural army that the eyes could not see. But Elisha saw it in faith. What can we learn from this? The Bible isn't saying that every time you pray this will happen. But don't underestimate God's promises from his holy Word. His protection is there whether you see it or not. But we must believe.

> Trust in the Lord with all thine heart; and lean not unto thine own understanding. In all thy ways acknowledge him, and he shall direct thy paths. (Prov.) 3:5–6

In my second book, *The Lord's Prayer Unveiled*, I have more information that reveal that God's angels are our servants only through Christ Jesus.

Our focus must be on the scriptures because it is the testimony of men who experienced his works, which builds our faith when we read them.

Here are a few scriptures on the invisible for our understanding.

> For by him were all things created, that are in heaven, and that are in earth, visible and invisible, whether they be thrones, or dominions, or principalities, or powers: all things were created by him, and for him. (Col. 1:16)

For the invisible things of him from the creation of the world are clearly seen, being understood by the things that are made, even his eternal power and Godhead; so that they are without excuse. (Rom. 1:20)

Now unto the King eternal, immortal, invisible, the only wise God, be honour and glory for ever and ever. Amen. (1 Tim. 1:17)

By faith Noah, being warned of God of things not seen as yet, moved with fear, prepared an ark to the saving of his house; by the which he condemned the world, and became heir of the righteousness which is by faith. (Heb. 11:7)

While we look not at the things which are seen, but at the things which are not seen: for the things which are seen are temporal; but the things which are not seen are eternal. (2 Cor. 4:18)

Read this chapter, and it will bless you. God does everything by faith before it comes into existence. Then it comes to pass, and he's trying to teach us the same way.

> Jesus saith unto him, Thomas, because thou hast seen me, thou hast believed: blessed are they that have not seen, and yet have believed. (John 20:29)

> [As it is written, I have made thee a father of many nations] before him whom he believed, even God, who quickeneth the dead, and calleth those things which be not as though they were. (Rom. 4:17)

These men and woman of God spoke in faith. They saw a nation delivered from their enemies time after time, the parting of the sea, countries destroyed because they fought against Elohim. They encountered healing, salvation, and provision when they leaned upon the Lord and not on themselves. They saw the impossible become possible. They learned the fear of the

Lord and at times forgot it. Yet when they sought after him, they experienced his love, mercy, and power once again. We can go on and on about what the *God of Israel and his Son* has provided for his people and the church.

And what amazing things are yet to come? It's definitely a blessing that we serve a living and invisible God.

When you study or read his Word, keep this in mind as you focus on the invisible to attain the visible by his power. To understand the fullness, put on the *whole armor of God* so that you may be able to stand against the cunningness of the devil.

We are in warfare daily, and as good warriors, we need to be trained. Know your enemy, know your armor, and realize that the battle has already been won. Believe it, accept it, confess it, and walk in it. Train others to join the army of the Lord.

> Thou therefore, my son, be strong in the grace that is in Christ Jesus.

And the things that thou hast heard of me among many witnesses, the same commit thou to faithful men, who shall be able to teach others also. Thou therefore endure hardness [endure suffer evil], as a good soldier of Jesus Christ. No man that warreth entangleth himself with the affairs [business, matter] of this life; that he may please him who hath chosen him to be a soldier. (2 Tim. 2:1– 4)

This is our confession; this is our belief and our battle cry.

Saying, Amen: Blessing, and glory, and wisdom, and thanksgiving, and honour, and power, and might, be unto our God for ever and ever. Amen. (Rev. 7:12)

Blessings, strength, and honor in Christ Jesus.

You can also purchase other books
written by William Chandler.
The Lord's Prayer Unveiled:
Reflections from the Mount
Beyond Paradise: The Story of
Our Ultimate Redemption